Shooting Two 2

A Story of Basketball and Friendship

by Jeanne Foley

Peppermint
BOOKS

www.peppermintbooks.com

DEDICATED TO THE MEMORY OF #12
BARB BONEFELD
1956-2010

ACKNOWLEDGMENTS:

Thanks are due to the many people who read drafts of this book including Mary Foley, Patti Good, Jamie Engelmann, Mary Vielbig, Nancy Van Gilder, Mary Pitchford, Mary Sachse, Paulette Valliere, Karin Allor Pfeiffer, Jo Ann Janes, Ari Austrins, Debbie Kruschwitz-List, the Bogan family, Katherine Dutton, Holland Griffin, Sharon Kjellberg, Sharon Krmpotich, and Carol Skay. For their lifelong support and encouragement, my loving thanks to four generations of Bratsch Babes, especially my sister Terri Foley who made this dream come true.

For additional copies,
visit www.peppermintbooks.com

PUBLISHED BY:
Peppermint Books
P.O. Box 16512
Minneapolis, MN 55416
Visit Peppermint Books at
www.peppermintbooks.com

Publisher: Terri Foley
Copyeditor: Sandy Whelan
Teen Consultant: Holland Griffin
Art Direction: Blue Tricycle, Inc.
Designer & Page Production: Blue Tricycle, Inc.

Publisher's Cataloging-in-Publication Data
(Provided by Quality Books, Inc.)
  Foley, Jeanne.
    Shooting two : a story of basketball and friendship /
    by Jeanne Foley.
    p. cm.
    SUMMARY: This girls' basketball novel follows a
    varsity team for a year as they train, practice, and
    compete in a small town in Minnesota during the late
    1980s.
    LCCN 2010942584
    ISBN-13: 9780982885215
    ISBN-10: 0982885210

    1. Basketball for girls--Juvenile fiction. 2. Girls
    --Minnesota--Juvenile fiction. 3. Friendship--Juvenile
    fiction. 4. Basketball stories. [1. Basketball for
    girls--Fiction. 2. Friendship--Fiction. 3. Minnesota--
    Fiction.] I. Title.

    PZ7.F7288Sho 2011   [Fic]
              QBI10-600254

TABLE OF
CONTENTS

GO THUNDERBIRDS!

CHAPTER ONE

"AT THE LINE FOR TORRINGTON IS *junior Barbara McMahon. Shooting two!"*

Barb wiped her hands on her shorts and took the ball from the referee. She took a deep breath, then flexed her knees. She bounced the ball in a slow rhythm: once, twice, three times. On the third bounce, she spun the ball so it came back up with the seams running straight across between her hands. A couple more backspins brought the black dot of the air valve into view. Her right hand slid across the leather, the index finger automatically finding and covering the dot.

The well-practiced routine worked its magic. A hypnotic calm blocked out the noise of the crowd, the pressure of the tie score, the 1989 state tournament berth at stake, the expectant looks of her Thunderbird teammates crouched along the free throw lane. Barb was on autopilot now.

Another deep breath. Bend the knees, bring the ball up, pull the right elbow in, right hand under the ball. Focus on the front of the rim. Another slow breath. Hold it. A split-second stillness, then the smooth launch. Knee and elbow uncoiling in synchrony, eyes locked on the rim, wrist pushing up and then flipping forward, fingertips grazing the grainy surface of the leather. Perfect backspin, perfect arch.

As the ball dropped softly over the front edge of the rim, a roar washed over the court. 58–57, eight seconds to go in the game, and now, a chance to put her team up by two on the favored Hunterville Tigers. Barb stepped back off the free throw line and turned to give a thumbs-up to Jamie Johnson behind her.

The ponytailed point guard grinned back at Barb, then caught the eyes of each of her three teammates crowding the lane lines. If Barb could just make this second free throw, the game—and the regional championship— was theirs.

Barb stepped back up to the line. The familiar pattern took over again. Wipe the hands. Get the ball. Bend. Bounce, bounce, bounce. Flip, slide, point to the dot. Breathe in, crouch, pause. Push up, use the legs, follow through. *Swish!*

Pandemonium. Whistle. Timeout. Hunterville's last one.

Coach Miller crouched in the center of the Thunderbird huddle, her piercing gaze riveting each player in turn. "Just like practice now," she demanded. "No fouls, no uncontested shots. All we need to do is slow Hunterville down, keep them off balance for EIGHT SECONDS." Coach Miller nodded to her assistant.

Coach Kelley moved to the middle of the huddle. "Remember now, number 13 looks to drive inside, but isn't a big threat from the outside," she began. "Back off a step to stop the drive, but keep a hand up just to keep her from launching one. Number 21's their gunner. Barb, you stick to her, keep the ball out of her hands, or smother her if she gets it." The coach looked around the huddle and locked eyes with Jamie. "Johnson, you go long, guard against the deep pass."

The head coach took over again. "I know you're all tired, but for eight more seconds keep moving those feet. Remember, we've got a two-point lead; they're the desperate ones here. If we don't foul and don't give them an open look from three-point range, the best they can do is tie. Now heads up, be smart, and let's go!"

The 11 blue-clad players crowded in around the coaches, right arms reaching in to the center of the huddle, hands stacked in a sweaty pile. Team captain Barb barked out, "On three, *defense!*"

The stacked hands bounced in unison. *"One, two, three, DEFENSE!"* The huddle broke, and five Thunderbirds hustled out to their assigned spots on the floor. The benchbound six strained forward in their seats, clasping hands in fervent grips, forgetting to breathe, eyes glued to the court.

A Tiger forward waited impatiently behind the endline. Finally the official raised her whistle to her mouth and handed the ball to the anxious inbounder. On cue, the big Torrington player in front of her jumped, whooped, and waved her hands in front of the passer. The Hunterville player hesitated, then leaned around the defender and pushed a sharp bounce pass to her point guard cutting up the middle. The clock started its countdown as the ball met the receiver's hands.

A Thunderbird guard quickly shifted over to cover the Tiger ballhandler. Barb backpedaled toward midcourt, in step with the sharpshooter number 21 streaking up the floor.

The Tiger point guard took one dribble, then another, but her defender cut off her move and forced her to pick up the ball. A quick pass snapped the ball back to the inbounder stepping onto the court. She immediately fired a baseball pass up the right sideline to Number 13, way out on the wing.

Jamie shot out to cover the receiver as she gathered in the long pass. Could there be any time left? Could she possibly make it from way out here?

Number 13 looked to drive left, but Jamie was all over her. A quick dribble to the right, then up with the desperation shot over Jamie's outstretched hands, just a heartbeat before the horn blared.

All other motion seemed frozen; all eyes tracked the path of the high-arching ball. A little off? Yes! A loud thunk sounded as the ball caught the rim and bounced straight up, then dropped back down to make a crazy circuit of the rim. The basketball seemed to hang forever there on the iron, balancing, balancing … And then … it teetered in.

Three points. Game over. Season ended.

Jamie slumped in disbelief out beyond the arc as jubilant Tigers leaped and hugged and celebrated all around her.

Barb made her way through the exultant throng to reach her dejected friend. With a protective arm around Jamie's sagging shoulders, Barb spoke urgently into the point guard's ear. "Hey, Johnson, you did just what Coach said. The odds of her making a shot like that, way out there, off balance, with you in her face … one in a million!"

Jamie shook her head. "I just can't believe it. We had it won!"

Coach Miller appeared and gave Jamie's arm a squeeze. "You couldn't have played it any better than that," the head coach said. She turned to beckon the rest of the straggling team, pulling them into a huddle to make herself heard over the raucous Tigers fans spilling onto the court.

"Now look," said the coach. "We just lost a tough game, but I've never been more proud of a team, *ever*. You never gave up, even when we were down by 12. Sure, we all feel rotten right now, coming so close, then losing on a crazy shot like that. But I want you to keep those heads up and use this game as our inspiration to work hard during the off-season. Remember— everybody from this team is back next year. Next season. Let's send our seniors off with the Thunderbirds' first-ever regional championship!"

Barb picked up the coach's refrain, pointing her finger to the net-cutting ceremony just getting under way out on the court. "*Next* March," declared the Thunderbirds captain, "they'll be watching *us* climb that ladder and cut down those nets."

The determination in her friend's voice lifted Jamie's slumping shoulders. "Guaranteed," she agreed. "And I'll bring the scissors." ◄

CHAPTER TWO

THE SUMMER HEAT ROSE IN WAVES from the worn black surface of the old asphalt track. The stiff brown grass of the infield prickled the sweaty backs of Jamie's legs as she finished up her stretching routine. Heaving a sigh, she hoisted herself to her feet.

Jamie made her way to the starting line marked faintly on the track in front of the faded wooden bleachers. She took off her Walkman, then bent to set her water bottle in the middle of the second lane. Straightening up, she took a deep breath and pushed a button on her wristwatch. Two beeps, all zeros. Ready to go.

Sweat was already trickling into Jamie's eyes. She pulled at the neck of her cut-off Thunderbird T-shirt, wiping her face with the worn cotton fabric. The sprints on today's training schedule would be tough going in this heat.

Jamie set herself for the first sprint. She leaned forward at the starting line, right hand at left wrist, finger poised on the start button of her wristwatch. At the beep of her watch she exploded off the line, knees lifting, arms pumping, eyes focused intently down the track.

She settled into a smooth, swift rhythm as she sailed around the first curve. Into the back straightaway she flew, eyes now trained on the pole marking the halfway point around the quarter mile oval. As she flashed past the marker, she stole a quick glance at her watch. So far, so good.

She throttled back to an easy jog to carry her back around to the starting point for the second sprint. As she trotted around the last curve, a glance at her wristwatch told her to slow down even more. Still she reached the starting line early, leaving seven seconds to dance lightly in place before bursting off on the second sprint.

By end of the sixth sprint, Jamie was sucking air in big gulps. Her legs felt heavy, and she didn't have to remind herself to slow down on the recovery jog. Her breathing was still ragged as she plodded around the far end of the oval. The start of the next sprint seemed to come much more quickly than after the first few. Still, she'd made all her target times so far. Only two more to go.

Sometimes she needed to remind herself why she did this. "This one's for the team, for the seniors," she silently declared. "For the fourth quarter of the last game in regionals, when we need our press. For us to be the ones jumping and hugging and cutting down the nets."

The memory of that loss was now four months old, but still plenty sharp to spur Jamie through her workouts. She thought of the pledge the team had made to get their seniors-to-be to the state tournament next year. She held on to that image as she felt her breathing ease, her heartbeat slow, the lightness return to her legs.

"OK," she told herself. "Go for it!"

Jamie slowed to a stop at the end of the curve. She paused just a moment to flex her knees and shake out her arms, then launched herself into her next furious dash down the track.

« « « T » » »

Barb leaned against the entry gate, watching the familiar sequence unfolding before her. As Jamie jogged up to her final sprint, Barb stepped into the tired runner's line of sight. "Come on, Jamie!" she hollered. "Last one. Be strong!"

Jamie gave her teammate a weary wave, then gathered herself for one last effort. "End of the game," she said to herself. She pictured the scene. Down by one. Six seconds to go. A rebound by Barb, a long lead pass ahead to Jamie. The victory depends on the strength left in Jamie's legs to push her ahead of the streaking defender to reach that ball, bank it in. Go!

As Jamie crossed the finish line, Barb fell into step beside her. "Nice job!" Barb exclaimed. "You were really in a zone on those sprints!"

Jamie only nodded, no breath yet available for speech. She knew her friend would stay with her for the two-lap cool-down jog; conversation could wait until her heart quit pounding and her lungs stopped burning.

Barb kept pace in a companionable silence through the first lap. Finally Jamie was able to spare some air. "Thanks," she breathed. "It's starting to feel... like I'm getting there..."

"Yeah, all this conditioning finally feels like it's beginning to pay off," answered Barb, adding, "But I'm glad I got up and ran early today, before the thermometer topped 90 and the breeze died."

The two girls finished out the last lap, then slowed to a walk. "Walk with me another lap, and tell me the scoop from your captains' meeting this morning." said Jamie, breathing a little easier now. "Did the coaches say anything about the newcomers trying out this year? Seems like there might be some serious competition for varsity roster spots."

Barb nodded. "No kidding. That should be a good thing, but I hope it doesn't end up causing problems for us."

Looking concerned, Jamie said, "I know some of the returning subs are really worried about the new girl that's transferring in from Iowa."

"Her name's Anna," said Barb. "Anna Kiefer. Sounds like she could really help us in the scoring department, judging by her stats from last year. I hear she's tough on defense, too—led her league in steals. She plays my position, you know. Personally I welcome the competition. The deeper we go, the more we'll be able to run."

Jamie knew Barb was right, but she didn't want anything to spoil their last year on the team together. "I wish you weren't graduating this year," Jamie said. "It's hard to imagine playing my senior year without you on the team, after all these years."

"Yeah," agreed Barb. "It's going to be weird going off to college in a year, maybe not even playing hoops at all if I go to a big school. But maybe I'll end up someplace close enough where I can at least get home to watch some of your games. And anyway, we still have a whole year before that happens. One last season to make good on all those plans we hatched way back in grade school."

Jamie smiled, picturing two little girls rehearsing the scene over and over again at the driveway basketball hoop. "Final game of the state tournament," she began. "Ten seconds to go..."

Barb picked up the play-by-play call. "... the Thunderbirds are down by one. McMahon pulls down the rebound, outlet pass to Johnson."

Jamie jumped back in. "Johnson dribbles the ball up the court, looks for an open teammate. Six seconds, five... Johnson looks left, looks right. Nobody open. Four seconds..."

"Here comes McMahon, trailing on the right."

"Johnson hits her with a perfect pass."

"The shot's up. The buzzer sounds..."

Jamie threw her hands in the air, triumphant. "It's good! Torrington wins the state championship!"

Barb stood up and bowed to the imaginary crowd. "Thank you, thank you."

Jamie reached up a hand, interrupting her friend's valedictory. As Barb pulled her to her feet, Jamie said, "Perhaps we ought to finish our pre-season training before you start practicing your victory speech."

"Yeah, I suppose you've got a point there..." Barb laughed. "Speaking of which," she said as she glanced at her watch, "it's almost time to head back up to the school for weightlifting."

"Race you to the parking lot!" challenged Jamie as she took off for the gate. «

CHAPTER THREE

IN ADDITION TO THEIR INDIVIDUAL WORKOUTS on the track, the team trained together three days a week during the summer in the school weight room. When Barb and Jamie got to the high school, the big twins Millie and Mollie Meyer waved from the small crowd of teammates already waiting by the back door to the gym. Greetings were exchanged as Barb produced a key from her pocket and opened the door.

As tri-captains elected by the team after last season, Barb and Millie and Mollie were responsible for running the off-season conditioning program. The three soon-to-be seniors gathered the rest of the group together at the end of the room, near the row of clipboards hanging from hooks on the wall. Millie spoke first. "OK, before we get down to work, anybody have any announcements?"

Jeri Swenson, a junior power forward and the champion lifter of the bunch, pointed to a box near the door. "The new T-shirts are in," she said, holding up a sample. The shirts were royal blue with bright gold lettering. The front read TORRINGTON GIRLS' BASKETBALL, 1989 DISTRICT CHAMPIONS. On the back was a picture of a thunderbird in flight, with the slogan SOARING TO NEW HEIGHTS emblazoned below it.

"When we're done lifting, you can each grab one and cross your name off the list," instructed Jeri. "And don't forget to drop by Barb's mom's store and thank them for sponsoring the shirts this year." A few puzzled looks on the younger girls' faces prompted her to add, "For those of you who are new, Barb's mom is the manager at Dillon's Sports Shoes in Barnesville."

"Cool shirts!" exclaimed Mollie. "Except next year they'll be saying Regional Champions."

"Or better yet, State Champs," countered her sister. "Hold that extra-extra-large for me," she added. "Any other announcements?"

Jamie raised her hand. "If anybody wants to get in some full-court running, my mom said we can ride along with her to Barnesville tomorrow.

"Mom's a biology prof at Shelby College," she explained to the newcomers. "She's going in to her lab for a few hours tomorrow, plenty of time for us to get a few pickup games at the outdoor courts on campus. Mom says we'll be back by suppertime, so you won't need to miss those hot Saturday night dates."

"Hot is right!" smirked Emma Larson. "I heard the air conditioning is out at the Bijou." Torrington's single-screen movie theater was the prime source of weekend entertainment in the small Minnesota town, at least for those without wheels to carry them to the Barnesville mall.

"Anyway," continued Jamie, "if you want to come, be at our place by 2:00

tomorrow afternoon."

Mollie stepped in to get the workout going. The girls spread out in a semi-circle on the floor around her and began the familiar stretching routine.

Ten minutes later the players were pulling their clipboards off the wall and dispersing to stations to set up for the first lift. Little was heard now except the clank of the iron plates and the whoosh of exhalations as players pushed the heavy weights. No time was wasted as they moved through the dozen lifting stations. After the first round, towels were retrieved, water bottles squeezed, and comments exchanged.

Marking the end of the three-minute break on the big wall clock, Barb hollered, "Round two. Let's get at it!" Around the stations they went again, almost balletic in their practiced movements. More clanking, a few grunts this time. Second set done.

"OK, three minutes rest again and then we push through this last set!" commanded Millie.

At each station a partner cheered the lifter through the last few reps. "Come on, Erin!" one spotter urged. "Just four more. That's it. *Seven … eight …* come on now, don't give up! *Nine.* That's it. Just one more now! I'm with you here. Come on. Up, up, up. Yeah! *Ten!* Good job!"

Finally finished, the players converged on the box of T-shirts by the door. The seven newcomers hesitated shyly in the wake of the varsity girls. Barb noticed their reluctance and waved them over. "Come on," she said. "You all are part of this club, too!"

The varsity hopefuls shot grateful glances at the co-captain and edged closer to the fray. "We weren't sure we were invited yet," said Amy Knudson, a gangly blond six-footer and captain of the eighth grade team last year.

"Yeah," echoed Kelly Carter, a compact little JV guard. "Since we weren't around when you put the order in, we didn't know if we were included."

Barb chuckled. "Mom figured we'd be getting some reinforcements, so she went ahead and ordered extra. Dig in!"

Jamie reminded the chattering crowd, "Don't forget about the road trip to Shelby tomorrow. Who's planning to come?"

Although many of the players already had weekend plans, four girls agreed to join Jamie and Barb. "Let's wear our new shirts," suggested Amy.

"Good idea!" agreed Barb. "Mom will be happy to hear the shirts were a hit." Emma, Kelly, Jeri, and Jamie agreed to the plan.

"Remember to be at my place by two," added Jamie. The others nodded, then headed out the door with shirts in hand.

Jamie lingered behind as Barb checked over the room. Each captain took the key for one of the three weekly sessions; Fridays belonged to Barb.

Barb finished checking all the clipboards while Jamie racked the last of the free-weight plates. Both girls grabbed towels to wipe down the lifting stations. Finally Barb looked around the room and was satisfied that they'd gotten everything back in order. "I've got Dad's car. You want a ride home?" offered Barb as she locked the door.

"Sure," said Jamie. "I don't know if my legs could get me home after running *and* weights this afternoon!"

Duffel bags in hand, the pair made their way out to the side lot where an old white Jeep was parked. The girls tossed their bags in the back and climbed into the front seat. With the windows cranked open, the ride down the hill from the school created a welcome breeze that ruffled their hair and dried the last of their sweat.

By the time they pulled into the Johnsons' driveway, Jamie had almost forgotten about her weary legs. She hopped out of the car and retrieved her gym bag from the tiny back seat. "See you tomorrow!" she hollered over her shoulder as she ran into the house. «

CHAPTER FOUR

JAMIE BANGED THROUGH THE FRONT DOOR, clattered into the kitchen, and dropped her duffel on the floor. The cool indoor air felt like heaven after the muggy heat outside. "Mom?" she queried.

"She's not home yet, and Dad had to run back to the office for a while," piped her little brother from the next room. Jason was 13 years old and still a runt.

Jamie strolled into the den where she knew she'd find Jason hunched over his new computer. "Did Mom say when she'd be home?"

Her brother pushed up his glasses, blinked, and finally replied without removing his gaze from the monitor. "She called an hour ago. They hit a snag calibrating some new lab equipment and she said she'd just have to stay till they got it straightened out."

Jamie peered at the computer screen that held her brother's gaze. "Maybe

Mom should have taken you with her. If it's a computer problem, I'll bet you could fix it!"

Jason blinked again and finally looked up at his sister. "Nah. It's something to do with oxygen tanks and hose fittings. Not my kind of hardware problem."

"Did Dad say what we should do for dinner?" Jamie called over her shoulder as she exited the room. "I'm starved!"

Jason emerged from the den and pointed to money on the kitchen island. "Pizza," he said. "Again." He poked at the bill with his finger. "Dad said we should just go ahead and eat, since he wasn't sure when he or Mom would get home."

"You want to call for it while I shower?" called Jamie as she started up the stairs to her room.

"I already did. Should be here by the time you're sanitized," quipped the bespectacled boy, pointedly sniffing the kitchen air.

"Oh, stuff it!" his sister threw back as she pounded up the stairs.

Jamie surveyed the disaster area that was her bedroom. A small desk and straight-backed chair were barely visible under a pile of clothing on the far side of the room beneath the window. "Jeez, I better do something about this mess," she said to herself. "You'd think Millie Meyer lived here!" The taller twin was famous for her untidy habits. 'Miss Entropy,' Jason had christened the Thunderbird center, using a term gleaned from his Encyclopedia of Physics. 'Mill-dew,' the team called her, in reference to a dead pair of socks once extracted from the depths of Millie's locker.

Jamie got out of her workout clothes and stepped into the shower. The hot water felt so good on her weary muscles that she lingered a few extra minutes under the soothing spray. Finally she'd had enough. Wrapping a towel around her long, wet hair, she went to search her room for her favorite pair of sweats. Her excavation successful, she tromped downstairs.

A flat cardboard box lay on the kitchen island. Aromas of pepperoni and tomato sauce sharpened Jamie's hunger. She flipped open the box, noting that two pieces were already missing.

From her chair on the porch Jamie could see across the big backyard to where it sloped down a hill to a small pond. A sleek Siamese cat sauntered in front of the view from the French doors. "Hello, Figgy," said Jamie. Figaro responded to Jamie's attentions with a yawn and a stretch. "Did I interrupt your afternoon nap?" The cat ignored her, staring regally out the window at his domain. Eventually he deigned to approach, allowing the girl to stroke his head in just the right spot between his dark ears.

The loud hum of a garage door intruded on the peaceful scene. A minute later Jamie's mother joined her on the porch, setting a briefcase full of papers on the wicker coffee table. "How was your workout today? I'll bet the track was sweltering."

Jamie nodded, working to swallow a mouthful of pizza. "I made it through the whole thing—and hit all my target times!" she reported proudly.

Mrs. Johnson smiled. "Good for you!"

"Did you get that equipment problem fixed at the lab?" asked Jamie anxiously. "I've got six of us lined up to go with you to campus tomorrow, so I hope you're still planning to go in to work."

"Yes. We finally figured out that one of the gas tank valves had a slow leak which was throwing off our calibration curves."

Jamie responded with a shrug. She finished off her pizza, then announced, "Hey, we got our new T-shirts today. Want to see them?"

"I'd love to!" replied her mother. "And you girls make sure you remember to thank Barb's mom. She went to a lot of trouble to persuade the owner of her shoe store to pay for them. She told me the whole story on our training run last Saturday."

An idea dawned on Jamie. "Say, why don't we stop by the store tomorrow on our way back from the college? We'll be in Barnesville anyway, and we're all going to wear our shirts for the pickup games."

Jamie ran upstairs while her mom fixed herself a plate of pizza. Jason joined his mother in the kitchen for the fashion show. Jamie slid back into the kitchen on her stocking feet, pirouetting to model both sides of the shirt for her audience.

"Doesn't that look nice!" exclaimed her mother.

Jason eyed his sister critically before adding, "Not bad, for jockwear."

"Thanks, Nerd Brain." Jamie flipped her hair over her shoulder and waltzed out of the kitchen.

"Don't mention it, Sweat Stain," Jason threw after her. ◀

CHAPTER FIVE

THE NEXT MORNING, BARB WALKED UP Jamie's driveway, savoring the fresh breeze. She tossed a pebble at Jamie's second-floor window, not really expecting a response. Seeing the open garage door, she found a beat-up basketball in its usual spot. A squeeze and two test dribbles told her it could use a little air. She located the pump hanging on the wall above Jamie's bicycle and gave the ball a few shots. A couple more bounces, a few more pumps, and the ball was pronounced fit for use. Barb dribbled the ball down the driveway and lofted a couple shots at the backboard looming over the edge of the wide cement driveway.

She was halfway through her warm-up routine when the Johnsons' front door opened and a tousled-looking Jamie stumbled out. Surveying her best friend's untucked shirt and untied shoes, Barb ventured a guess. "Just get up?"

Jamie yawned sheepishly, then nodded. She laced up her scuffed Adidas Superstar hightops, then stood under the basket for ball return duty. When Barb finished her warm-up, the girls switched places.

A fierce game of one-on-one followed. Since neither player would call a foul, contact escalated until the contest was finally interrupted by a small voice. "You guys going to kill each other?"

The combatants halted, panting and laughing simultaneously. "You want to ref?" asked Barb.

Jason shook his head so hard he nearly lost his wire-rimmed glasses. "No way!" he exclaimed. "Do I look that stupid?"

"Hardly," responded Barb. "Everybody knows you're smarter'n Einstein."

"Oh, please," groaned Jamie. "Let's not feed that little ego."

The exchange was cut short by the appearance of Jamie's mom at the front door. "What time did you tell the other girls to be here?" she called across the lawn.

"Two o'clock," answered Jamie and Barb in unison.

"Good—just enough time for lunch. Come on in then, before the food gets cold."

By the time the girls emerged from the house after lunch, Amy and Kelly had arrived and were shooting around at the driveway hoop. A few minutes later, a big Swenson's Dairy Farm truck rumbled around the corner. Sun glinted off the gleaming silver milk tank as the passenger side door swung open and a tall, muscular girl sprang out.

"Thanks, Dad!" Jeri waved as the truck pulled away. "Hi, gang!" she said to the assembled quartet.

"Quite the limousine!" remarked Amy.

"Well, when you live on a farm, you hitch along with whatever's going to town."

Emma's bike jumped the curb and skidded to a halt just short of the group. "Hi, guys! Hope I'm not late."

"Nope. We're just getting ready to load up the car," said Jamie. She climbed into the rear of her mother's old station wagon and unfolded the back rumble seat. "Going to be a tight squeeze," she warned. "I guess Kelly and I get to sit back here where there's no leg room."

"And Amy can have the front seat so she's got room for those stork legs," offered Barb. "That leaves me and Jeri and Emma in the middle seat. Gym bags on laps, everyone!"

Mrs. Johnson slid into the driver's seat as the girls finished their seating arrangements. "Got room for my briefcase back there?" she asked Jamie.

"Sure, Mom. Hey, Kelly, maybe you could sit on it so you can see out the window!"

The little guard gave Jamie a friendly poke. "I don't think I *quite* need a booster seat, thank you very much!"

Finally the crew was settled in and buckled up. Jason waved from the front steps as the car rolled out of the driveway. "Remind your father to be home by six," called his mother through the open car window. "We'll pick up dinner on the way home."

"OK. Don't forget dessert!"

The 15-mile drive to Barnesville flew by on a wave of chatter. Tall stone buildings soon came into view atop a hill in the distance. At a granite marker engraved 'Shelby College,' Mrs. Johnson turned the car onto a tree-lined lane leading up the hill. As the road crested the hill, a right turn brought the science center into view. Mrs. Johnson pulled the station wagon into a parking spot at the rear of the building and the girls piled out.

A tall woman in a white lab coat looked up as the group entered the lab in the basement of the building. "Good morning, Dr. Johnson," she said.

"Hello, Karin," replied Jamie's mother as she plucked her own lab coat from its hook behind the door. She gestured at the girls. "You know my daughter Jamie, and you may remember Barb, Jeri and Emma from the games you came to watch last year." The three varsity veterans waved to the lab assistant. "And these two are Amy and Kelly, the long and short ends of the new recruits." To the players she explained, "Karin's a graduate student working on a master's degree with me. She's also assistant coach of the women's basketball team here at Shelby."

Jamie nodded. "Yeah, and she started for the U on a full-ride basketball scholarship!"

"And she had a tryout for the U.S. Olympic team," added Jamie's mom. "So if you girls have any basketball questions, now's the time to get them answered. If you can stick around for a few minutes while Karin helps me set up the experiment, I could probably spare her for an hour or two."

"Great!"

"Cool!"

The girls milled around the lab while the two women fiddled with valves and hoses. Before long all the equipment was ready to go, and Karin gathered the group over by the door.

"What time should we head back here?" Jamie asked her mother.

"Oh, let's say around 4:30. That gives you almost two hours to run the court and still leaves us enough time to stop by Dillon's on the way home. The shirts look great, by the way."

"Hey, Jer," said Barb. "Didn't you bring a spare one?"

Jeri nodded and dug around in her duffel bag. She pulled out an extra-large blue shirt and handed it to Barb.

Barb presented the shirt to Karin with a flourish. "Here," she said. "Kind of a thank-you in advance for showing us the ropes."

Karin accepted the gift and held it up to her shoulders. "Gee, thanks!" she said. "But you're the ones who did *me* a favor by getting me out of work," she added, with a wink at her boss.

"Don't mention it," said Jamie. "Besides, now we can use you as our secret weapon in the pickup games!"

"I sense an ulterior motive here," commented Dr. Johnson.

Karin grinned as she shucked her lab coat and pulled on the new shirt. "Hey, at least it fits!"

Her boss just shook her head. "See you in a couple hours then. Good luck!" «

CHAPTER SIX

KARIN LED THE BLUE-SHIRTED BAND across campus to an asphalt court behind the Student Union building. A lively game was raging up and down the court. A ragtag group of challengers lounged in the grass along the sidelines.

"Looks like mostly townies today," observed Karin. "High school guys from Barnesville, probably."

Leaning against the pole at the far end of the court was a bored-looking guy wearing a green Shelby College T-shirt with the right sleeve cut off. "Hey, A.J.!" Karin called to him as she approached the court. "How's the competition looking today?"

"Hey, Karin." The scraggly-bearded man unfolded himself from his slouched pose and sauntered over toward the group. "Not much doing yet," he said, nodding his head toward the court. "A little early for the regular crowd, plus it's the weekend, so lots of the Shelby guys are off campus. I got out of work early, so I thought I'd come over and get in a little warm-up running with the children."

"Who's got next?" asked Karin, glancing toward the small crowd of boys lining the side of the court.

"Me and those five guys on the end," A.J. said, pointing with his chin. "They just got here, and I talked them into letting an old man run with them for a game or two. Those other guys there just lost the last game. Guess you're third in line after them." A.J. glanced dubiously at the six girls ringed around Karin. "You playing today or just coaching?"

"I might play a little, if one of my Thunderbirds here needs a rest." Karin pointed to her new shirt. "I just got made an honorary team member. Jamie here is the daughter of my boss at the lab, and these girls are from her high school team at Torrington. They're pretty tough—your guys might just need you on the court if you're going to have a chance against them!"

A.J. harrumphed and said, "Yeah, right!" Just then the game ended and he was called out onto the court to join the challengers.

As they watched the next two games, Karin gave her eager players some instructions on the unwritten court rules. "We play one point per basket; first team to 10 wins."

Jamie interrupted: "Don't you have to win by two?"

"Not here," answered Karin. "That can make the games go on too long, and the challengers don't like to sit on the sideline forever."

Karin resumed her lecture. "Winning team keeps the court, of course, and the winners get first possession in the next game, too. Call your own fouls, but if you want to be taken seriously, just push back and keep playing unless you're bleeding bad."

Amy sat up and swallowed hard. Karin looked at her and cracked a smile. "I'm just kidding—about the bleeding anyway. But seriously, you want to hold your ground out there. If there's a blatant foul, go ahead and call them on it, but otherwise just keep going and make up for it on the other end."

The girls turned their attention back to the court to size up the competition. A.J.'s team easily won the first game and was leading 3–1 against the second team of challengers when Karin resumed her tutorial. Gesturing toward the court, she said, "You'll notice these guys are mostly run and gun. Not a lot of passing or team play. Now they might be a little stronger and quicker than you are, but if you stick to your teamwork and fundamentals, you can hang with them."

"How do you think we should match up with them?" asked Barb. As the lone senior present, she automatically stepped into her captain's role. "We've got two point guards, Jamie and Kelly. Hey, Kelly—besides the one position you played some two on JV last year, too, didn't you?"

Kelly hesitated. "Uh, I'm not sure what a two is," she admitted.

"Me either," added Amy.

Barb launched into a quick explanation. "The number system is based on offensive roles. A 'one' is the point guard, the director of operations out on the court. The 'two'-guards are the shooting guards, good ballhandlers and good shooters. A 'three' is the small forward, kind of a swing position between guard and forward. The 'fours' are power forwards—more like centers, but they usually play mostly facing the basket and maybe a little farther out than the centers or post players, the 'fives.' Fives are the big girls who roam around the lane with their backs to the basket."

Seeing that her explanation satisfied the two newcomers, she asked Kelly again, "So you played some at the two spot?"

The muscular little sophomore nodded. "Quite a bit, actually," she said.

"OK. That gives us a pair of two-guards we can go to—Emma, plus Kelly if we need her there. Emma's 5'8" and can play either shooting guard or small forward, which is also my position. But I can handle the ball okay, too, if I need to switch from my usual three spot to a two. I've played a little power forward, too, but we're in pretty good shape there at the four position with Jeri." Barb turned to Amy and said, "You played mostly five last year, didn't you?"

"Yeah," replied the skinny six-footer. "I can play power forward in a pinch, but mainly I'm a center."

"So there you have it, Karin," concluded Barb. "We've got all five positions pretty well covered, but we could use some advice on matching up against their guys."

Karin surveyed the six girls, then turned toward the court. A.J.'s team now led 6–3 and appeared well in control of the second game. "Well, looks like we know who we'll be playing, anyway," she commented as she turned back toward the girls. "I've played against A.J. a lot, and I think you can handle him just fine, Jeri. Remember he's a lefty, although he can go to his right OK, too."

Karin continued, "That little guy in the black shirt with the wolf on it looks like their floor leader. Notice that he's *very* right-handed. Whoever's on him, most likely Jamie or Kelly, should try to force him to his left. Doesn't look like anybody out there on defense has really noticed that yet, so ol' Mr. Wolfman's probably used to getting away with it."

Jamie and Kelly watched the court and nodded thoughtfully.

"What about that other guy, out on the wing?" asked Jamie, pointing to a chiseled blond boy sporting a lifeguard tan and wearing a white Nike muscle shirt. "He looks like he can shoot the lights out!"

"You're right; he's got a nice touch from long range," agreed Karin. "But notice that he only hits when they give him plenty of room." She looked at Barb. "He gets flustered if you crowd his shot. Got that, Barb?"

The captain gave a thumbs-up sign. Then she gestured toward the court, indicating a medium-sized fellow wearing running shoes and a well-worn purple Barnesville track singlet. "What about him? He doesn't seem to get the ball much."

Karin glanced at the court and then over at the lone sub, also sporting a track shirt. "Yeah, looks like running and rebounding is about all those two get to do out there, and only one of them's ever in at a time. I'd say you can get away with sagging off of them and playing some help defense, or even double teaming on Buff Boy or A.J."

The two guards laughed, looking forward with relish to trapping the two self-styled stars of the asphalt.

"OK, that leaves their center, the dude with the maroon University of Minnesota basketball camp shirt." Karin pointed to the tall, skinny fellow camped out in the key. "He might be their weakest link. Amy, even though that string bean must be at least 6'4", I'd say your best bet is to front him, muscle him away from the ball. Then when a shot goes up, slide around him fast and box out hard. Rebounding's going to be a key.

"I saw your team last year in regionals, and you did a great job of calling 'shot' on defense and hustling to box out. Just do the same thing here. If all five players remember to block out, these guys won't know what hit them. But remember—you'll have to take some pushing and banging to hold your block-outs, so spread your feet wide, keep your butt low, and stick those elbows out."

When the game ended 10–4, the five Torrington girls walked out onto the court. The boy in the wolf shirt stood at half court with the basketball, which he dropped casually at Jamie's feet as she approached. Jamie deftly scooped up the ball, then looked around to make sure her teammates were set to play defense. Satisfied, she flicked the ball back to Wolfman and hollered, "Ballgame!"

The boy stood dribbling as he surveyed the court. Buff Boy popped out to the wing and called insistently for the ball with his outstretched hands. The point guard faked a pass his way, then hit A.J. coming off a screen set down low by the purple-shirted trackman. Jeri slid through the screen, but not in time to keep her man from getting off a shot. *Swish.* 0–1, townies.

Barb grabbed the ball and stepped behind the endline. Jeri and Amy took off down the sides of the court, leaving Jamie and Emma to vie with their defenders for the inbound pass. Trackman and Wolfman were pressing hard, hoping to fluster the girls into a quick turnover.

Emma cut hard toward the ball. Jamie started to do the same, then quickly reversed direction and sprinted up court. Barb hit her right in stride with a lob pass over the top. As Jamie neared the painted three-point arc, Amy and Jeri crossed underneath the basket. Stringbean and A.J. had them covered, so the girls cleared out of the key. Realizing she still had a step on Wolfman, Jamie drove hard to the hoop. Layup. 1–1.

Karin and Kelly cheered from the sidelines as the Thunderbirds raced back down on defense. This time down, the muscle-shirted blond got his way and got the ball. Barb stepped up in his face, challenging him to shoot over her. One fake. Two. Give up and pass off? Hardly! As Buff Boy heaved up an off-balance 25-footer, Barb screamed, *"SHOT!"*

Immediately, Barb and her four teammates stepped toward their players. Almost in unison they pivoted in front of them and sealed them away from the basket. Five pairs of arms went up, five sets of knees bent low. A shove in the back by A.J. nearly sent Jeri flying, but she held her ground. As the ball bounced off the backboard toward her, Jeri leaped and wrenched it out of the air with both hands.

The dozen or so boys awaiting their turn from the sidelines whistled and clapped. "Hey, man," one of them jeered at A.J.'s team, "you gonna let those girls whup you?"

A furious A.J. dogged Jeri hard, clipping her arm as she aimed a chest pass at her outlet. The ball deflected toward the Stringbean, who picked it up and banked an unguarded shot off the backboard and in.

"Hey," protested Jeri.

"Yeah, what?" A.J. challenged her back.

Shaking her head, Jeri picked up the ball and tossed it to Barb waiting out of bounds. "Never mind," muttered Jeri. "Let's go, girls!"

The blue-shirted five worked the ball patiently on the next possession. Finally Emma broke free on the right baseline, just in time for an overhead pass from Amy at the high post. An easy 12-footer. In … and out. Trackman snagged the rebound, and it was off to the races again. Alley oop to Stringbean, over Amy's head. Dunk. 1–3.

"Timeout!" yelled Karin.

"Timeout?" A.J. shook his head in disbelief. "What are you talking about?"

"New rules," said Karin.

"Says who?"

"Says me. One per team per game. Called when you've got the ball, or when it's out of play."

"What the—"

"Come on, guys," cajoled Karin. "Afraid a little strategy will outsmart you?"

The boys grudgingly agreed to the conditions. Karin pulled her charges over for a quick huddle. "You see how tight they're crowding you on defense?"

The girls nodded emphatically. "Yeah, they're practically inside our shirts!" griped Jeri.

Amid the resulting giggles, Karin continued. "You can use that to your advantage. Remember that backdoor play you ran at the end of the regional finals? Well, that's open all day, the way they're jamming you so close. Jamie, you need to set them up with a good fake pass as your teammate cuts toward you. When the defender lunges for the steal, your cutter takes off hard behind him toward the basket. Backdoor, bounce pass, bingo."

"Got it!" Jamie clapped her hands. "Come on, gang! Let's give these bozos a run for their money! On three—*fight!*"

Hands pushed in and covered Jamie's. "*One, two, three, FIGHT!*" The huddle broke. Emma joined Karin pacing the sideline, replaced by Kelly on the court.

The Thunderbirds ran their plan to perfection. Barb burned Buff Boy for the first backdoor layup. After holding the boys scoreless on the next possession, Jamie hit Emma on the other side. Another easy shot, and Emma put it home. 3–3.

A brick by A.J. led to a perfect fastbreak off a rebound by Jeri. Swanson to Johnson to McMahon. 4–3.

"Timeout!" His black shirt stained with sweat, Wolfman halted play.

As the boys groused at each other under their basket, Karin slapped Jamie on the back. "Way to go, Ace!"

"How about subbing for me?" Amy asked Karin.

"You tired already?"

"No, but—"

"Well then, stay out there. You girls are doing fine. I want to see you win this without me. Besides, I didn't bring my hoop shoes and I'm not sure I trust my battered ankles in these," Karin pointed to her running shoes.

"Well, okay …" said Amy.

The game resumed. Trackman Junior inbounded the ball to Wolfman, who pushed it up the court to Buff Boy. Barb rushed him, but he got off a shot—no, a lob pass to Stringbean. Amy was fronting him as ordered, but the taller boy reached over her head from behind and grabbed the ball. The sideline boys whooped as the ball clanged through the rim. Tie score at 4.

Kelly brought the ball up as Jamie and Barb tried to shake free on the wings. Something different was going on—a zone? Sure enough, the boys had set up in a two-one-two with Stringbean clogging the middle. Kelly passed to her right, shifting the zone. A quick skip pass back to the far side. Jump shot, Barb. 5–4, Thunderbirds.

That proved to be the high point of the game for the blue-shirted girls. The boys rallied for four unanswered scores. Jeri finally countered with a little jump hook over A.J., but that was all they got the rest of the way.

Final score: 6-10, townies.

The girls trooped dejectedly over to Karin as the next team of challengers rotated in.

"Hey, why the long faces?" demanded Karin. "You all did a good job out there!"

"Yeah, but we lost," griped Amy. "That big skinny guy must have knocked the ball away from me 10 times. What a klutz he is! He'd have fouled out twice already if this had been a regular game with refs."

"You just need to get a little meaner, that's all," replied Karin unsympathetically. "On offense, seal him out with your hip and an arm, and call for the ball away from him with your other hand." Karin demonstrated using Jeri as her defender.

Amy looked unsure. "How about getting out there next time and showing me for real?"

"Well, I guess I could use a little workout," sighed Karin. "OK. I'll play a few points, but then you're right back in."

Amy agreed happily. The team turned their attention back to the court, where A.J.'s boys were walloping the challengers even worse than they had the time before, setting up the rematch the girls had been waiting for.

A.J. eyed Karin as she took the court with the blue team. "Momma gotta rescue her little girls?" he sneered.

"Hey, I'll sit out if you do!" she threw back. "Maybe we should let the high-schoolers settle it between themselves."

The bearded man shook his head. "Nah, I need to get a good run in today. Can't come tomorrow."

Play resumed, the pace as furious as in the first contest. Karin was clearly winning the battle down low with Stringbean. A.J. called for a defensive switch, but he couldn't stop her either. By the time she subbed out for Amy, the Torrington blues led 7–3. Final score: 10–7, Thunderbirds.

Buff Boy slammed the ball down in disgust. "Rematch?" he snapped.

"Not so fast," came a shout from the sideline. "You can wait your turn like the rest of us!" One team of challengers had stayed to watch the girls beat A.J. and the Barnesville boys.

The Torrington girls dispatched the challengers with relative ease, winning 10–5 on some hot shooting by Jeri and Barb while Karin cheered from the sidelines. Jamie looked at her wristwatch: 3:50. Time for one more game before they had to head back to the lab.

A.J.'s team jumped up from their perches on the sideline. As he led his troops onto the court, A.J. directed a question toward Karin. "Shirts game?"

Emma did a doubletake. "Shirts and skins? We can't—"

Karin interrupted. "No, he means we play for our shirts. Winners get the losers.'"

"Uh, we can't do that," said Barb.

"You afraid you gonna lose?" Buff Boy flexed in his Nike tank.

"No way," Karin defended her girls. "It's just that they just got these shirts from sponsors, and they wouldn't be too pleased to see them on your scrawny backs instead of theirs."

"Well, if they win, they won't be," Wolfman shot back. "Y'all should be willing to take the chance with those tacky T-shirts."

"*Tacky?*" Barb's eyes flashed as she checked her teammates' faces. "Well, ladies?"

"I say go for it," said Jeri.

"Me, too," said Emma.

Kelly wasn't so sure. "But what if—"

Jamie cut her off. "If we lose 'em, we lose 'em. But we won't. So let's go."

With that, the rubber match was on.

"So, A.J.," called Karin. "We in? Or do we leave it to the kids?"

"You kidding? I'm getting one of those 'tacky' T-shirts!"

"OK, you asked for it!"

Amy and Kelly gave way to Karin and the varsity veterans to start the game. Wolfman tossed the ball to Jamie and yelled, "Game!" Three minutes later the score stood at 3–1, blue shirts up. Jamie felt a little shiver of relief as she pushed aside the vision of showing up at her mother's lab in her sports bra.

Trackman Senior inbounded the ball to Wolfman, who hit a breaking A.J. with a baseball pass downcourt. Jeri had him step for step, forcing him to pull up short of the basket. Jeri held her ground, refusing to leave her feet for the fake she knew was coming. Sure enough, he pulled the ball back and pounded down a dribble. A hand flashed out behind him. Emma poked the ball away just as it came up off the floor. Karin snatched up the loose ball and whipped an outlet pass to Jamie.

Jamie swung automatically into the well-practiced fast-break drill. Bring the ball up the middle, pull up at the free throw line, keep your dribble going, scan your two wings. Nothing open. OK. Look for your own shot. Covered. No problem—here comes the trailer—and it's Karin! Toss her the ball, stand back and cheer. Up she goes—*oh, no!*

Karin crumpled to the asphalt and grabbed her left ankle. "Arghhh!" she grimaced. "I knew these shoes would get me into trouble!"

"Hey, I didn't—" began A.J.

"No, it's not your fault," said Karin. "I just stepped on your foot and rolled my ankle over. Nothing I haven't done before. But I'm afraid I'm out for the day."

Kelly ran to the Union for a bag of ice. Meanwhile the game resumed with Amy in the lineup replacing Karin. The girls did their best to shake off the loss of their not-so-secret weapon, but suddenly every bounce seemed to go against them. The jubilant boys ran off six straight baskets. 3–7, townies. Bye-bye, shirts?

"Timeout!" Karin sat up on the sideline and shifted the ice bag off her foot. "Get over here!" The startled Thunderbirds jogged over to Karin's side as the injured woman struggled to her feet. "Amy, Jeri—what happened to those post moves?" she scolded. "Come on, you two held your own just fine last game when I subbed out, didn't you?"

The two girls looked at each other, then at their teammates. Amy spoke up first. "I need some help back there on defense. That tall guy just keeps reaching over my head and grabbing the ball."

Jeri had an idea. "Maybe you'll have to quit fronting him, Amy. Guess they finally figured out how to get him the ball. But if you can set up behind him, maybe Barb or Emma can help you out with a double team, or at least sag in a little and jam up the passing lanes. I'll get ready to cover the dump-off to A.J."

"Sounds good," said Karin. She looked around the huddle. "You aren't about to concede those nice new shirts to these guys, are you?"

"No way!" came the response.

"Okay then, get back out there and show what you're made of!"

The recharged girls surged back out onto the court. The boys, smelling a win, were waiting in a full-court press. Barb held up four fingers, hoping her teammates would remember the special press-breaker the coaches had taught them during the playoffs last year. She saw Jeri pull Amy over for a quick conference. Yes! There they were, all four lined up across the court in front of her, even with the free throw line.

A.J. kept his boys up close, cutting off all the passing lanes. "Good, it's working!" thought Barb. She smacked the ball, and four blue shirts sprinted toward her. As she jabbed the ball toward them, they each jammed out a foot, then took off streaking down toward their own basket. Four parallel lines—one had to be open.

Barb pulled the ball back behind her ear, then fired a baseball pass down the right side. Jeri looked like a wide receiver as she gathered in the basketball. Up came Buff Boy to stop the ball. Jeri led the wide-open Jamie with a bounce pass to the left side of the lane. Layup. 4–7.

Hustling back on defense, the girls forced A.J. to launch a long shot. The Thunderbirds slammed into their blockouts, then leaped fiercely for the rebound. As they raced back up court, Jamie noticed that the boys had returned to their tight man-to-man defense. A cut, a fake, and a backdoor pass made it 5–7.

The teams traded baskets on the next four possessions to bring the score to 7–9, townies ahead. On the next possession, Emma tripped bringing the ball up the court. Turnover—boys' ball. Game point coming up.

Wolfman walked the ball up the court, directing traffic as he came. He noticed his center was no longer being fronted and sent a pass in to the middle. A waiting Emma streaked in from the right wing to steal the ball. Up ahead to Jeri. Good, for 8–9.

Taking a gamble, Jamie lurked under the basket as her teammates scrambled back on defense. A.J. took the inbound pass from Junior Trackman, then turned to bring it up court. Jamie reached in from A.J.'s blind side and tapped the ball away. Barb raced up to recover the loose ball and tossed it back to a waiting Jamie. Bank shot—missed!

A wild scramble for the rebound. Jeri muscled it away from Stringbean, put up a shot. It was good! 9-9. Next basket would win it.

Wolfman took the inbound pass this time, careful to look around before he dribbled it up the floor. He saw the tall girl behind his center again and lofted him a lob pass. Stringbean caught the ball and turned to the basket. Amy held her ground. Stringbean brought up an elbow and bowled her over. *Score!* 10–9! Townies won the game!

"Hey!" yelled Amy, wiping blood off her split lip. "Foul!"

"*What?*" Stringbean was incredulous.

"She's got a point," admitted A.J. "You do that to me, I'm calling it, too."

Red-faced, Stringbean went along with the call that canceled his winning basket.

Thunderbirds' ball. Barb to Jamie. Jamie brings it up. Passes in to Amy at the high post. Pivots. No shot there. Across to Emma on the wing. Jeri posts up on A.J. down low, seals him off, calls for the ball. Bounce pass to her low side. A.J. slides over to cut off her turn to the baseline. Jeri spins back to her right, lofts a little hook with her left hand, over Stringbean, up and over the rim.

Basket good! *Game over!* «

CHAPTER SEVEN

JAMIE'S MOM LOOKED UP FROM HER DESK as a clamor at the door broke the cool silence of the lab. Six tired but smiling girls spilled in through the door behind Karin.

"How'd you do at the—Say, what happened to you?" Mrs. Johnson eyed Amy's swollen lip.

"Ah, that's nothing, Mom," cracked Jamie. "You should see the other guys!"

"Yeah, we beat the shirts off them!" added Amy, causing a burst of hysterical laughter from her teammates.

A quizzical look from her boss prompted Karin to explain. "We ran into a crowd of boys who needed a little lesson."

"Oh?" Mrs. Johnson crossed her arms and leaned back in her chair with a tell-me-more/this-had-better-be-good look on her face.

Barb took over the story. "Well, we got into a game with these guys from Barnesville High."

"Yeah, 'townie' boys," interjected Kelly.

"I see you've been tutoring the girls in the campus vernacular," noted Mrs. Johnson, aiming a wry look at Karin.

Karin blushed, then gestured toward the sweaty group. "They gave the guys a good game their first time up, but they couldn't quite pull out a win. I gave them a few pointers, though, and they came out and beat them the second time around."

"Yeah, and they weren't too happy about that!" Jamie's claim was seconded noisily by her teammates.

"And then …?" Mrs. Johnson tapped a pencil on her desk blotter.

"And then we beat the next guys," said Jeri.

"And then the first guys bet us their shirts that we couldn't beat them a second time," added Emma.

"They bet you their shirts. Hmmm. And what did you girls put up as collateral?"

Jamie eyed her mother sheepishly. "Uh, well …"

Karin came to her rescue. "For the really big challenge games, local custom says that the cost of losing is the shirt off your back. I could hardly let the girls look like they didn't have confidence in their game. Besides, I knew they'd defend their honor."

"Yeah, and we all had on sports bras anyway, so it's not like we'd have been indecent or anything." Jamie's rationalization drew a frown from her mother.

"Anyway, it all worked out in the end," Karin added quickly. "Amy saved the day by standing tough and taking a big charge at the end of the game."

A blushing Amy fingered her split lip, then rushed to spread the credit. "And Jeri came through with the winning basket after the foul gave us the ball back."

Karin stepped back in with a suggestion. "Let's show Dr. Johnson the spoils of your victory." As the girls dug though their duffels, the graduate student gave her boss a wink and a high sign. She was rewarded with a resigned sigh and a shrug of the shoulders.

The girls lined up to display their damp prizes. Amy was particularly proud of her maroon and gold Minnesota Gophers shirt; the memory of seeing Stringbean's skinny bare chest more than made up for the pain of her fat lip. Emma and Kelly showed off their purple Barnesville track singlets, and Jeri modeled A.J.'s one-sleeved fashion statement in Shelby College green. Barb held her white Nike muscle shirt up to her chest, while Jamie proudly flaunted the black wolf shirt.

"Well, girls, I think it's time to pack up and head for home," said Mrs. Johnson. "We've still got time for a quick stop at Dillon's, although your nice new shirts look a little the worse for wear."

"At least everyone will know they're getting put to good use," offered Jeri. "Hey, everybody, just be sure to keep your arms down at your sides." Emma sniffed her armpits, producing another fit of laughter from the group.

A few minutes later the Johnsons' station wagon turned onto the main street in downtown Barnesville where a small shoe store stood between a cafe and a bakery. Jamie's mom headed across the street in search of take-out for dinner. Barb led the troops through a heavy glass door upon which the words "Dillon's Sports Shoes" were painted in black letters edged with gold. A bell sounded, catching the attention of a petite woman perched on a stool behind the counter. "Hi, Mom!" called Barb.

"Well, hello!" said Mrs. McMahon as she dismounted her stool and stepped back to view the team. "Don't you girls look nice!"

A tall, balding man emerged from the stockroom at the back of the store. "Well, Maggie!" he boomed. "So these are the famous Thunderbirds you talked me into outfitting." He surveyed the disheveled lineup. "Not bad, not bad!" he concluded.

"Thanks a million, Mr. Dillon," said Barb. "These shirts are the coolest!"

"And we just broke them in against some Barnesville boys up on The Hill." added Jamie.

"Did they bring you good luck?" asked Mrs. McMahon.

"Absolutely!" replied Jeri. "We took them two out of three!"

The girls buzzed excitedly with the news of their victories. Amy proudly displayed her battle scar while her teammates regaled the store staff with a lively account of her game-saving feat of courage. By mutual agreement from a conference in the car, however, they shrewdly avoided mentioning their shirt wager in front of Mr. Dillon.

The bell above the door jingled again. "Hello, Maggie!" Mrs. Johnson greeted Barb's mother with a hug. Then she extended a hand to Mr. Dillon. "And John, so good to see you. The girls were determined to stop by and show you their new shirts. We're all so grateful to you for donating them."

Mr. Dillon waved off her thanks. "Oh, don't mention it, Katie. I'm always happy to back a winner."

"Well, I'm afraid we have to scoot. I promised to have the girls back to their families by 6:00, and my husband and son are probably wondering where their dinner is. Goodbye, Maggie; bye, John. Thanks again for your generosity!"

The girls echoed their thanks as they streamed toward the door. Out on the sidewalk Barb informed her teammates, "You'll have a little more room on the way home. I'm going to stick around and drive home with Mom."

Emma reached in to the middle seat to grab Barb's gym bag. "Don't forget to pull out that stinky shirt when you get home," she said to Barb. "I'm sure it needs some airing out!"

"No doubt!" agreed Barb. "*Major* airing, plus a disinfectant treatment!" As her teammates laughed, a thought struck the captain. She pulled Buff Boy's sweaty white shirt from her bag, holding it up gingerly with the tips of two fingers. "Hey, let's wash these up and wear them to weightlifting on Monday."

"Good idea, Buff Girl!" Jamie gave her best friend's biceps a squeeze. "But you'll need to up your bench press poundage to fill out that nice muscle shirt!"

Mrs. Johnson started the car. As it pulled away from the curb, Barb hollered after them, "Go, Thunderbirds!" Cheers and whistles erupted from the car. As the station wagon picked up speed, sweat-stained banners of gold, maroon, purple, and black unfurled out the windows. Barb lifted her damp white prize off her shoulder and waved it in response as the car sped out of sight. ≪

CHAPTER EIGHT

THE SCHOOL CORRIDORS BUZZED WITH TALK as students milled around looking for old friends and new lockers. Jamie slammed her locker door and went in search of Barb.

"Hey, McMahon—happy first day of school!"

"Hey, yourself, Johnson. Ready for the fun to start?"

Jamie grimaced as she hefted her bulky book bag. "Well, I don't know about trig and physics, but I'm excited to finally get onto the court for captains' practices."

"Me, too," said Barb. "Conditioning is one thing, but I'm sure itching to get back in the gym next week. Millie and Mollie and I are meeting with the coaches during our third-period study hall to run through some ideas for drills and scrimmaging."

"Did you find out when we have the gym yet?" asked Jamie. "I know volleyball gets it right after school, but I'm hoping we can sneak in after them instead of at the crack of dawn like last year."

"That's one of the things we'll find out at the study hall meeting. Just for you, I'll do my best to push for afternoons!"

A bell sounded, signaling five minutes till the start of class. Jamie sighed. "Well, off to History of the Western World. See you at lunch?"

Barb nodded. "Yeah. Usual table. Spread the word."

By lunchtime, news of the impromptu gathering had spread through the team grapevine. Nine of the returning 11 varsity players had trickled over to the designated table by the southeast windows of the cafeteria.

"Where are the twin titans?" Jeri asked Barb.

"They're still in the coaches' office," answered the co-captain. "Coach Miller was just finishing showing them part of a post moves video-tape from a camp she worked at this summer. It had some drills she wants you tall types to work on this fall at captains' practice. They'll be here shortly."

"*Shortly?*" quipped Brenda. "Not likely!"

Amid the yelps and groans evoked by Little B's pun, the Meyer sisters appeared at the table. "What's so funny?" asked Millie.

"You don't want to know," advised Bernie. "Short girl humor. Sick."

While their teammates finished eating, the three seniors gave a quick report on their meeting with the coaches. "Captains' practices will start next week, on Tuesday," announced Mollie. Cheers erupted around the table.

Looking apologetically at Jamie, Barb added, "They'll run Tuesdays and

Thursdays from 6:45 to 8:00 … in the morning. Sorry, Jamie!"

Jamie buried her face in her arms and groaned.

Barb hastened to explain. "We figured that way we could still keep up our weight training a couple days a week right after school." As her friend slumped over her empty lunch tray, Barb plowed ahead. "There is some good news, I promise."

Jamie peeked one eye over her crossed arms. Barb continued, "The coaches said that we can cut back our track workouts to one day a week."

"Oh, joy," came the muffled response as Jamie dropped her head back down.

"Come on, gang," urged Jeri. "Fire up! This is our year, remember?"

"Yeah," said Tina. "This is what we've been working for all summer. You know it'll pay off when regular practices start in November, and games in December."

"And playoffs in March!" chirped Bernie.

"Okay, okay." Jamie picked her head up. "Just don't expect me to be Miss Cheery-Face at seven a.m." Heaving a sigh and straightening her shoulders, Jamie turned to face the twins. "So give us the rest of the scoop," she commanded. "Anything new and different on the early-morning agenda this year?"

Mollie set down her glass and wiped milk from her lips. "Mostly the same stuff as last year. The new freshmen and last year's JV-ers will be there, of course. Since the coaches can't be in the gym till regular practices start, the 11 of us veterans will take turns reffing scrimmages. With all the new kids coming in, we should have enough to run two courts at a time."

"Speaking of new kids, has anybody talked to that new girl who just moved here from Iowa?" asked Emma. "I hear she's quite a hotshot."

"Coach Kelley mentioned her," said Barb. "She's just a sophomore, but I guess she played varsity since seventh grade down there."

Millie nodded. "Yeah, not only played, but made All State as freshman ... *and* All Conference as an eighth grader."

"Yeah, but what's the competition like down there?" retorted Tina. "She comes from a pretty small town, right? They must be like Class Z or something." Tina's comment drew a burst of laughter.

Mollie stepped in to caution her teammates. "I wouldn't write her off just yet, gang. They take their basketball seriously down there in Iowa. Mom said she remembers seeing the Iowa girls' state tournament on TV up here in Minnesota, even back in the dark ages when she was in high school. Anyway, we need to make this new kid feel welcome, and if she can help us win games, I say great!"

"What position does she play?" asked Emma.

"Mostly three," said Barb. Emma relaxed at this news until Barb added, "Well, I think they said she played some shooting guard, too."

"Did the coaches say how many they're planning to keep on varsity this year?" Emma couldn't quite keep a note of tension from creeping into her voice.

"Ah ... well, no, not exactly," said Millie. "Last year, you remember, they only kept 11. But other years they've had as many as 13 on the roster. So it could be anywhere in there. Guess it just depends on how tryouts go in November."

The lunchroom huddle broke up as the warning bell sounded for fourth period. "You planning to run after school?" Barb asked Jamie as they gathered up their lunch trays.

"Yup," replied Jamie. "I'll meet you down at the track."

⊰«⊰«T⊱»⊱»

A few hours later the two girls sat stretching on the dusty infield of the track. "At least it's cooled down since the weekend," commented Jamie.

"Yeah," agreed Barb. "It sure was a scorcher for that race our moms ran on Saturday. A half marathon—13 miles! Can you imagine?"

Jamie shook her head. "Not for me, thank you very much!"

The girls finished their warm-ups and headed out onto the track. Forty minutes later they flopped back down on the grass, spent and sweating.

"So, what are your latest predictions for tryouts this year?" Jamie asked Barb. "Like I said before, I know some of last year's subs are worried about getting cut this season …"

"Yeah, I know Emma's anxious, especially with that new girl Anna coming in."

"And you said she plays mostly the three spot?" asked Jamie.

"Primarily, but also some two," replied Barb. "That would be my spot and Tina's out of last year's starters. And we *do* need a stronger bench. Remember last year we only went eight deep in games most of the time. You at point, Tina at shooting guard, me at small forward, Mollie at power forward, and Millie at center. Then Jeri subbing in at the four spot for Moll or sometimes at three for me. Bernie backed up Mill at five, and Brenda spelled you and sometimes Tina at the one and two positions."

Jamie continued the lineup rundown where Barb left off. "The others didn't really get in much. You're right. We didn't have a really solid backup at either shooting guard or small forward. Emma and Erin are hard workers and great to have at practice, but they really didn't click with the offense last year when they did get in."

"I know," said Barb ruefully. "But I hate to think of either of them getting cut ..."

"Well, they both sure did work hard on their conditioning this summer," said Jamie.

Barb nodded, adding, "And Emma looked pretty good in our pickup games at Shelby in July, didn't you think?"

Jamie agreed, mentally replaying the outcome of the now-legendary Shirts Game. "Yeah—especially that one steal she had against A.J. in the last game."

Barb returned to the roster rundown. "That just leaves Lu Ann from the returning eleven. She's a junior, too, and hardly played at all last year. And her spot, the two-guard, is where we really need some backup."

Jamie nodded thoughtfully. "LuAnn was gone a lot this summer, too. Wasn't at lifting practice much. But then neither was Tina, since her softball team was travelling so much all summer."

"Yeah, but Tina's a natural. I mean, she plays shortstop on one of the best summer fastpitch teams in the state. Not to mention the fact that she was a starter on the basketball team last year despite being the only freshman on varsity." Barb ticked off the names on her fingers. "So that gives us eight fairly solid returning varsity players and three questionables. Plus Anna, who could even be a contender for the starting lineup, much less just making the varsity."

Jamie gave her friend a sharp look. After a short silence, she changed topics. "How about the new kids coming up from JV and last year's eighth grade team?"

"Well, of course you know Amy and Kelly pretty well from summer lifting and the infamous pickup game. Amy's kind of skinny for a center, but she worked hard on the weights all summer."

"Unfortunately, that's probably the position we're best stocked at already," commented Jamie.

"True," said Barb. "There's Mill, of course. And Bernie—well, even though she's not the most coordinated athlete in the world, she *is* six foot three."

"How about Kelly? I thought she did a pretty good job at point guard against Wolfman when she subbed in for me this summer," said Jamie. "And she's a pretty sweet shooter, too, even if she is a little small for a shooting guard."

Barb nodded her agreement as she took another long pull from her water bottle. "Let's see, who else has been showing up in the weight room this summer?" she asked, wiping her lips.

"Well, I'd say that those two kids from JV, Drew Smithson and Katie Doherty, might be possibles," said Jamie.

"And Drew's a two-guard, and Katie can play either one of the forward spots, so they might have a legit chance."

"Think any other freshmen besides Amy have a shot at making varsity?"

Barb thought for a moment. "The only other one I can think of would be Jenny. Jenny … What's her name?"

"Uh … Olsen, I think."

"Yeah. She's a forward, too, if I remember right."

"Wow, so that makes … how many?"

Barb ticked off the players on her fingers. "Um … 17."

Jamie whistled. "Whew! Should make for some tough battles at tryouts!" Pushing down on Barb's shoulder, she levered herself to her feet. "Race you to the locker room!" «

CHAPTER NINE

AN EARLY-SEPTEMBER DAWN was just breaking as a line of cars deposited yawning girls at the side door to the high school gym. Jamie and Barb trudged up the sidewalk with their gym bags slung over their shoulders. "Just think," muttered Jamie, "if we had wheels we could have slept in for another 20 minutes this morning."

"Ah, come on now," Barb chided her grumpy friend. "It wasn't even a mile, and the walk's a good warm-up for practice." As they approached the small crowd milling around outside the gym, a light blinked on above the side door.

Barb greeted the janitor as he pushed open the heavy metal door from the inside. "Hi, Mr. McMillan!"

"Mornin', gals. Up before breakfast, aren't you?"

A bleary-eyed Jamie nodded her head woefully. "Ain't that the truth! But hey, thanks for letting us in—I think …"

"Aw, don't mention it. You can pay me back by winning the state title next March."

Bernie clumped in behind Jamie. "You bet, Mr. McMillan! And you better be right there cheering us on!"

"Never miss a game," he replied. "Took the whole family up to your regional tourney last year. Thought for sure you had it won there in that last game, coming from behind like you did." He shook his head and sighed. "New year now, though, eh?"

Bernie nodded and followed Jamie into the gym. More players straggled in as the captains unlocked the equipment room and pulled out a cart of basketballs. The other veterans herded the newcomers over to the bleachers. An expectant hum of voices accompanied the tugging off of sweats and the lacing up of shoes.

"Hey, nice shirt!" Jamie croaked, pointing to Amy's maroon Gophers basketball camp T-shirt.

The tall freshman flushed at the attention, then grinned shyly at the older girl. "I'm glad to see you had the same idea," she said, eyeing Jamie's wolf shirt. "Think they'll bring us good luck?"

"Hope so! Or at least more than they brought those poor boys!" exclaimed Jamie. She tugged at the fabric, eyeing the wolf logo on her chest.

A purple-shirted pair joined their laughter. "Kelly called me last night to remind me to wear mine, too," said Emma, pointing to their hard-won apparel. "And I see old A.J.'s Shelby shirt made it here, too."

Sensing their attention, Jeri sauntered over to model her single-sleeved green shirt. "I hope this doesn't cool down my hot shooting," she cracked as she flexed her bare right arm. As Barb approached the group, Jeri called out, "I see you chickened out and wore a T-shirt under yours."

"Yeah," replied Barb, glancing down at the blue T-shirt sleeves protruding from the ample armholes of her white Nike tank. "I was afraid you'd all be too dazzled by my Buff Girl arms to concentrate on practice!"

Mollie interrupted the resulting guffaws with a sharp whistle blast. "OK, everybody, listen up!"

The hubbub in the bleachers faded as the three captains stood in front of the hopeful throng of faces.

"Some of you already know the routine," said Mollie. "But for those who weren't here last year, welcome to captains' practice. You probably all know that coaches aren't allowed to run practices till the official start date of …" She looked to her sister for help.

"November 15th," filled in Millie.

"Yeah. So until then," Mollie continued, "we'll have the gym twice a week to introduce everybody to our team drills and get in some scrimmaging to work off that summer rust."

Barb stepped forward. "But first we want to have everybody introduce themselves, since we've got some new faces here. I'm Barb—Barbara McMahon. I'm a senior and a tri-captain along with our other two seniors here, Mollie," gesturing to the slightly smaller twin, "and Millie Meyer."

Millie waved and took over the introductions. "Why don't we start over on this side. Just stand up and give your name, year, height, and position. Oh yeah, and I'm a 6'1" center, my sister here is a 6'0" forward, and Barb is a 5'10" forward."

Two dozen girls stood and recited in turn. Then all eyes turned curiously to the dark-haired girl at the far end of the bleachers. She got lightly to her feet. "Anna Kiefer," she said quietly, then paused. "Tenth grade. 5'9" forward," she finished, then sat back down.

Millie took over again. "OK, gang. Time to get to work. After today, soon as you come in you can grab a ball and warm up on your own for the first 10 minutes or so. Then stretching and a few drills, followed by scrimmaging till practice ends at 8:00."

Barb glanced at the big, wired-caged clock high on the north wall. "Since we're getting a late start today, let's take just five minutes to shoot around before we stretch."

The 28 girls dispersed among the four baskets on the two full-courts and the six auxiliary backboards bolted to the side walls. Basketballs hit the floor in an uneven rhythm, punctuated by the sharp screech of rubber soles on polished hardwood.

Jamie dribbled her ball over toward the side basket where Anna stood alone lofting free throws. "Mind if I join you?"

"Be my guest," said the new girl without interrupting the rhythm of her shots.

Jamie picked up her basketball and held out her hand. "Jamie Johnson," she said.

Anna swished a final free throw, then reached over to shake the offered hand. "Anna Kiefer," she replied as she retrieved her ball.

"Welcome to Torrington," said Jamie. "I hear you're from someplace in Iowa," she commented as she banked soft shots off the right side of the backboard.

"Uh-huh," answered Anna, dribbling her ball in a low figure eight around her legs.

Jamie moved to the left side of the basket, continuing her warm-up shooting. She tried again to get a conversation going. "So, how do you like it up here so far?"

"It's OK, I guess," replied Anna as she spun the ball effortlessly on her index finger.

A whistle interrupted the exchange. "Come on." Jamie waved Anna over toward the center circle of the main court. "Stretching time."

Barb led the awakening crowd through the team's usual stretching routine. As the girls clambered to their feet after the final exercise, Barb called out, "Everybody take two laps around the gym."

As the players lumbered into motion, Barb fell into step beside Jamie at the rear of the pack. "Thanks for going over to shoot with Anna, Jamie."

"Hey, it was the least crowded basket," replied her friend with a still-sleepy grin.

"Anyway, thanks," said Barb as they continued their leisurely warm-up jog. "Your taking the lead should help break the ice with the others. I just want to make sure we don't make her feel like an outsider."

The three captains put the players through a round of defensive shuffles and a passing drill, then divided the big group into three smaller ones for a rebounding drill. Twenty minutes later a line formed at the water fountain. An impatient Jamie waited in line, jiggling her arms and rolling her head around to work the kinks out of her neck. She turned to Tina standing behind her. "So what do you think of the new kid?"

"She's not too bad," admitted the sophomore. "But she's gonna have a run for her money if she thinks she's going to beat out Barb for a starting spot!"

Jamie bent to slurp thirstily at the fountain. She straightened up and wiped her dripping chin on her shoulder. "Not happening!" she exclaimed. "Next?" While Tina took her turn, Jamie continued her commentary on Anna. "She does play tough defense, though. I saw her poke the ball away from Bernie a few times."

"I noticed that, too. She's sure got quick hands. I bet it's a while before poor Bernie puts the ball on the floor again!"

Jamie sniffed and said airily, "Big girls always want to dribble too much, anyway."

"How true!" answered Tina with a snort.

A whistle knifed through their conversation.

"Well, time to act like a striped shirt," said Jamie. "Catch you later."

Jamie relieved Barb of her whistle and grabbed a game ball. A quick conference with Bernie determined who'd cover which end of the court, and the second scrimmage was under way.

By the time the wall clock showed 8:00 a.m., a sweaty but animated bunch was heading for the bleachers to pull on their sweats. Millie raised her voice over the chatter. "Nice job, everybody! See you day after tomorrow, same time, same place." «

CHAPTER TEN

BY OCTOBER, the morning convoy of cars was dropping players off at the gym in total darkness. A few weeks later, darkness still reigned even when morning practice ended. A restlessness spread among the players as one week blended into the next. The routine was growing old. And the tension was growing, too. Tryouts week was fast approaching.

Barb nosed her mom's van into a slot in the dark parking lot. "Wake-up call!" she announced.

Jamie stirred in the front passenger seat. "We there already?" she croaked, stretching and yawning. "I was just starting a good dream."

"Looks like we're a little early," noted Barb. "Mr. McMillan hasn't turned the door light on yet."

"Jeez, I could have stayed in my nice warm bed for a few minutes longer."

"Yeah, but if I hadn't gotten Mom's van today, we'd have been walking like usual, and you'd have had to roll out even earlier."

"Yeah, I guess." said Jamie, looking unconvinced. Switching gears, she posed a question to Barb. "So what do you think's going to happen in tryouts next week?"

"Got me," replied her friend with a serious look on her face. "Still looks like 17 or 18 people have a reasonable chance at making varsity. And you know we can't have near that many—"

A knock on the steamed-up window startled both girls. Two tall forms lurked outside in the dark. Barb rolled down her window. "Mornin', gals! Up before breakfast, ain't ya?"

The Meyer twins laughed as they piled into the back seat. "Brrrrr!! Mollie shivered. "That's a wicked cold wind out there!"

"Basketball weather!" crowed her sister. "Finally!"

"Jamie here's been pumping me for information about cuts," reported Barb. "Thinks the coaches tell us everything."

"Well, Jamie, join the guessing club," said Mollie. "We've kind of hinted at the subject with the coaches, but they haven't given us any clues as to their grand plan for the lineup."

Just then the gym door light flicked on, illuminating a small huddle of their teammates waiting with warm breath steaming and cold feet stamping. "Time to make some muscle heat, girls!" exclaimed Millie. "Only one more morning practice after this one."

"Hallelujah!" hollered Jamie.

The four veterans rolled out of the van and reached the door just as it swung open. "Morning, gals," came the greeting from the janitor. "Up before breakfast again, eh?" «

CHAPTER ELEVEN

THE NEXT MONDAY THE WEAK afternoon sun filtered through the glass block windows high on the south wall of the gymnasium. The familiar sounds of bouncing balls and screeching soles seemed more subdued and tense than usual as the players ran through their warm-up shoot-around. The girls tried not to look at the four clipboard-carrying coaches perched on the top row of bleachers.

"Looks like we've got tough decisions to make this year," commented Sharon Miller, the head varsity coach. She glanced sideways at her staff as they surveyed the action on the floor below.

"Yeah, but we can't really complain—looks like we should have the athletes to field two great teams this year," replied her assistant, Randi Kelley.

Louise MacDonald, the head coach of the junior varsity, nodded in agreement. She turned to the dark-haired coach beside her. "What do you think, Cody?" she asked her new JV assistant.

Coach Tyler tapped a pencil on his clipboard a few times before answering. "Cuts are going to be tough!" he finally replied.

The four coaches continued to watch from their lofty vantage point as the three captains herded the scattered shooters together at center court for stretching. "Well, time for my first speech of the year," said Coach Miller to her cohorts. She rose from her seat and started to make her way down the bleachers.

Down on the floor, Barb and the Meyer twins led an unusually quiet group through their standard stretches. A few freshman eyes flicked nervously toward the coaches approaching across the court.

The players finished their final stretch and started to scramble to their feet for the customary warm-up laps. Coach Miller motioned them to stay seated, then cleared her throat.

"I know we're all a little wired today," she began. "At least I know *we* are." The other three coaches standing outside the circle of seated girls nodded and smiled, each waving in turn as the head coach made the obligatory introductions. Formalities completed, Coach Miller returned her attention to the intense expressions still firmly fixed on the faces of the players.

"This is what we've been waiting for ever since last March," she said, gesturing to the court around them. "I think we all know that we have the chance to be part of something special this year. I have *never* come into a season feeling more excited than I do right now, this season, with this team."

She paused briefly, looking into the upturned faces. "Yes, it's true that we can't have 28 players on the varsity roster." No one moved a muscle. The coach clasped her hands behind her back and cleared her throat once more.

"By the end of this week, we'll have to make some tough decisions, to split this group up into varsity and JV. Friday after practice we'll be deciding on rosters, and each of you will get a call that night from one of us coaches. I want you all to know my door is open this week and anytime during the season. If you're concerned about something, or want to know where you stand, just come on in and talk."

The coach checked her wristwatch. "OK then, enough speechmaking. Let's get cracking. After your two laps, we'll divide up for position drills on the main court. Guards with Coach Kelley under that basket over there, forwards with Coach MacDonald right here at midcourt, and centers with Coach Tyler at the other basket. Everybody up and let's get moving!"

The girls bounded to their feet, glad to put their pent-up energy to use. After an uncommonly rapid warm-up jog, the players dispersed to their designated groups.

Twenty minutes later, a shrill blast from Coach Miller's whistle halted the activity. "OK, free throw drill," the head coach boomed. "Split up into groups of no more than three, one group to a basket. Everybody shoots 10 free throws, two at a time, then rotate. Keep track of your makes and report them to Coach Kelley when you finish."

Jamie snagged a ball and rounded up Barb and Tina to shoot with her. As Tina started her free throw routine, Jamie stood along the lane line next to Barb. "So how're the forwards looking?" asked Jamie.

"Pretty impressive," answered Barb. She stepped up to retrieve the ball as it swished through the net. Barb flicked a chest pass to the shooter, then turned back to Jamie beside her. "Anna's giving me a run for my money. I can see why she made all those All-Star teams down in Iowa."

Jamie looked at her friend for a moment. "You aren't really thinking she might knock you out of your starter's spot, are you? I mean, you *were* our second-leading scorer last year, and besides, she's just a sophomore."

Barb saw the worried look on her friend's face. "Nah," she laughed. "I can take her. Don't worry. But we sure won't have to worry about backup at the forward spot this year."

Tina dropped her second free throw cleanly through the hoop. As she stepped off the line to make way for Jamie, Tina added her two cents. "She plays a pretty good two-guard, too. Maybe I'm the one who should be worried!"

Jamie scooped up the ball and dribbled up to the free throw line. Her first shot fell just short, but as soon as she let the second one go, she knew it was good. "You're up, Barb," Jamie called out. "Game's on the line. Down by one. One-and-one. Don't choke now!"

Tina and Jamie kept up the chatter to force their teammate to concentrate. Barb calmly lofted the first shot softly over the front of the rim. "Tie score! McMahon at the line!" whooped Tina, picking up on Jamie's imagined scene. "Chance to win the game now, Mac—keep us out of overtime!"

Barb wiped her hands on her shorts and got set once more. Up and in. "My hero!" swooned Tina.

Barb grinned and stepped off the line. "Your turn again, Teenie. Keep that perfect string going, now!"

The threesome finished up their free throws and went over to report their results. Coach Kelley was just finishing up with the previous group. " ... and Kiefer, 10 for 10. Nice job there, Anna!" The coach looked up at the approaching trio. "Let's see ..." she said, looking down at her clipboard. "OK, hmm ... guards ... Here we are. Johnson?"

"Seven," answered Jamie.

"Behrens?"

"Nine!" said Tina.

"OK ... hmmm ... forwards—McMahon?"

"Ten for ten, Coach!" reported Barb.

"Nice work, girls," said the coach. "You can grab a quick drink. Then meet back up at center court. We'll be dividing into two groups for some full-court passing drills."

Another hour flew by in a flurry of drills, punctuated twice more by free throws. Half an hour to go. Scrimmage time. "OK, folks, listen up for your teams," ordered Coach Miller. She read off four lists of seven names.

Coach Tyler tossed out two game balls, then joined the other coaches as they made their way back up to the top of the bleachers. Coach Miller pushed the timer button on her sports watch and the four coaches settled in to watch the action on the two scrimmage courts.

"I see you split up the veterans today," commented Coach Kelley, making a notation on her clipboard.

"Yeah," replied the head coach. "There were some matchups I really wanted to see."

"Like McMahon on Kiefer?" asked Coach Kelley.

"For example," affirmed Coach Miller. "Guess you saw what I saw when you were working the forwards on their position drills, eh?"

"Yup," answered her assistant. "Not that we'll probably have to worry about that pair as far as cuts go, but it looks to me like we might have a battle for a starting spot on our hands."

"Well, it's a little premature to speculate on that just yet," cautioned the head coach. "But that certainly is one of the matchups we want to keep an eye on." The four coaches watched intently as the games picked up speed.

Ten minutes later, Coach Miller stood and up and blew a blast on her whistle. "Rotate courts!" she shouted through her cupped hands. As the players regrouped, the coaches scrambled to finish scribbling down their observations from the first scrimmage.

Two more rounds and the final whistle sounded. "That's it for today, girls," came the announcement from the bleachers. "Excellent practice! Let's see more of the same tomorrow."

«« « 𝕋 » »»

Thursday evening found Jamie sprawled in a faded green overstuffed chair in the corner of Barb's little attic bedroom. Her right leg hung over one arm of the chair as she rubbed the other leg with both hands. "Jeez!" she exclaimed with a grimace of pain. "I didn't think I'd get so sore again after all the workouts and captains' practices we did this fall!"

Barb regarded her friend from her perch across the room. Leaning against the wall with her legs stretched out across the width of her twin bed, she, too, was massaging her aching thighs. "Yeah, but an hour or so twice a week in the morning's not the same as two-plus hours four days in a row. And somehow I suspect we might be going at it just a *little* harder now that we're into tryouts."

Jamie threw her friend a suspicious look. "You saying we were dogging it at those crack-of-dawn practices?" she challenged. "Speak for yourself, woman!"

Dodging the pillow that zinged her way from the vicinity of the green chair, Barb defended her comment. "I'm just saying that the stakes are higher now, and maybe people are just squeezing a little more out of their tired bodies this week. Got to impress the coaches, you know."

Jamie sighed and turned her attention to her other tender leg. "Well, I guess we'll all learn our fates tomorrow night. Any predictions, Captain Mac?"

Barb gave her friend an exasperated look. "You never give up, do you?" She plumped up the projectile pillow and stuffed it behind her head.

"So who do you think's gonna get the bad news?" Jamie persisted. "Think they'll drop any of the veterans down to JV?"

Barb sighed in frustration. "I'm telling you, I don't know any more than you do, Jamie."

"So guess," commanded her friend. "I'll start: Anna's in."

"Oh, tough deduction!" interjected Barb.

"A little worried, are we?" said her friend sweetly.

Barb crossed her arms over her chest. "No, but thanks for asking." She made a face in Jamie's direction. "She's definitely going to help us this year, though, and if that means less playing time for me, I'll deal with it. Just 'cause I'm a captain doesn't mean I can't sit the bench some. I'm not conceding the starting three spot to her, mind you—not by a long shot. But there's a long way to go before that gets decided."

"Not really," countered Jamie. "Only about two weeks till the first game."

The downstairs door opened and a head poked into the stairwell. "You girls ready for some dessert?"

"Yeah, Mom," answered Barb. "What is it?"

"Homemade apple pie," answered Mrs. McMahon.

Jamie sprang up from her chair, only to grimace when her stiff legs hit the floor. "Sounds good to me—we'll be right down!" she hollered in the general direction of the stairwell. She reached over to pull Barb to her feet. "Come on, Gimpy," she said. The two girls hobbled gingerly down the stairs. ❰

CHAPTER *TWELVE*

COACH MILLER GAVE A NOISY SIGH as she pulled the office door shut behind her after Friday's practice. Muted sounds of showers spraying and locker doors slamming drifted through the walls from the adjacent locker room. Sounds of voices were conspicuously absent; none of the usual after-practice horseplay was evident today, the last day of tryouts.

The head coach plopped down in her chair and propped her feet up on a dented gray desk. The chair springs squeaked as she swiveled around to face the three other coaches jammed into the small office. "OK, folks, down to business," Coach Miller said as she uncapped her pen.

She pulled two blank pieces of paper off her clipboard, carefully folding each in half. As she ripped each sheet neatly down the crease, she instructed her staff: "Let's start by each listing all the players we believe are definitely out of the running for varsity. Then we'll compare lists; any players on all four of our lists will be taken out of the pool."

"How many should we list?" asked Coach Tyler as he passed the half-sheets of paper around to the other coaches.

Familiar with the annual routine, Coach MacDonald answered her assistant. "No set number. Just any kids you're sure wouldn't be contributors on varsity."

Coach Miller elaborated, "We've got 27 players to consider tonight. I thought maybe we'd lose more than just one this week, but Lu Ann's the only one who bailed out."

"So how many will you keep on varsity?" the JV assistant continued his questioning. "I mean, will we cut anybody totally, or do we keep everybody on JV who doesn't make varsity?"

"I like to keep the varsity roster to no more than 12," answered Coach Miller. "More than that and there's not enough playing time to go around. On JV you can usually handle a few more—and if we end up cutting any upperclassmen from the varsity, they may decide not to play at all if JV is their only option."

"Yeah, that's true," said Coach Tyler. "I hadn't thought of that."

"OK. List your definite no's first," said Coach Miller, taking up her pen and clipboard. "And no peeking—everybody draws up their own list."

Each coach scribbled quickly at first, then paused to consider the last few names. The silence was broken only by the occasional squeak of a chair and thoughtful taps of pencils on teeth.

Finally Coach Kelley stood to gather up the finished lists. She handed the papers to Coach Miller, then walked over to the shiny whiteboard on the wall and picked up a blue marker pen.

As her assistant wrote the heading "JV Squad" on the far left side of the board, the head coach unfolded the slips and lined them up side by side on the desk surface. She slowly read off the names of the girls appearing on all four lists as Coach Kelley wrote them on the board. When she was finished, 11 names were neatly written in blue.

"Well, that's a start," said Coach Miller. "That leaves 16, from which we need to cut at least four more. We'll do the next easiest step now—list your definite varsity keepers." She passed out another round of papers and the four coaches bent to their task.

Ten minutes later, nine names stood written in red under the heading "Varsity Squad", on the opposite side from the blue list. Coach Miller eyed the two columns of names and sighed again. "Well, now that we're warmed up, it's time to earn our pay."

Coach Kelley was busy constructing five rows down the middle of the board, labeled with the position numbers one through five. She knew the next step would be to consider the remaining candidates against the team's needs at each position from point guard to center. She entered the nine varsity definites in red first, then added the remaining seven names in green in a second column. She also put stars in front of the names of last year's returning varsity players and underlined the returning starters.

DEFINITES:

1. *Jamie Johnson, *Brenda Thorson
2. *Tina Behrens
3. *Julie McMahon, Anna Kiefer
4. *Mollie Meyer, *Jeri Swanson
5. *Millie Meyer, *Bernie Luskey

MAYBES:

Kelly Carter

*Emma Larson, Drew Smithson

*Erin Melby, Jenny Olsen

Katie Doherty

Amy Knudson

"OK, gang," said Coach Miller. "Now comes the tough part. Out of those seven players on the right, we can keep only two or three. They're all good kids, good players, hard workers. There's no ideal system for this part, so let's just try to break down our needs and also try to think about how our decisions might affect the team's chemistry."

Coach Kelley chewed pensively on the end of her green marker as she looked at the list of names. "Well, one thing's for sure," she said finally. "It's definitely going to affect morale if we drop either of those two varsity veterans on the Maybe side of the list."

"Yeah, I've been thinking that, too," said Coach MacDonald. "Not that you'd want to keep Emma or Erin on varsity just for that reason, if it meant sacrificing talent in a position where you need help."

Coach Tyler nodded his agreement. He jotted a couple notes on his clipboard, then flipped back to look at some observations he'd recorded during the long week of tryouts. Finally he looked back up at the marker board and offered, "Well, maybe if we're going to look at our needs by position, we could start with the five spot. Looks like we're pretty well set at center. Both Millie and the Luskey girl are pure post players, and you'd generally play only one of them at a time. And if you need a second backup, Jeri Swanson can play center almost as well as Bernie."

"Yeah," echoed Coach MacDonald. "What we give up in height, we'd make up in hands."

"Hey, now," retorted Coach Kelley. "I've been working with Bernie on that. She hangs onto that ball a heck of a lot better than last season!"

"Ahem!" interrupted the head coach. "Are we agreed, then, that the five position is covered?"

"Well," said her assistant, "I hate to cut that Amy Knudson. She's only a freshman, and sort of on the skinny side, but she's a quick learner, and comes ready-made with good hands."

Coach MacDonald spoke up. "But it probably would be better for her overall progress if she could stay with us on JV for a year and get more playing time, rather than ride the end of the bench for the varsity."

"True," agreed Coach Miller. "And we could always bring her up with us at the end of the season for playoffs and get her a little varsity experience to carry her into next year." The other three nodded. "So we're all agreed then. Knudson to JV and keep just Meyer and Luskey at center?"

Three heads bobbed again, and Coach Kelley swiped an eraser through the last row under the Maybes. Knudson was added to the blue JV list at the left.

Coach Tyler leaned back in his chair and heaved a throaty sigh. "Whew!" He stretched his arms and peered at the marker board. "So that's one down. Where do we look next?"

"Looks like we'll need another two-guard," said Coach Kelley. "Tina's great, but we can't have her on the floor the whole game every night."

Coach Tyler ventured tentatively, "Well, the new girl did play some two down in Iowa last year, from what you said. And with McMahon return-ing, it's going to be tough getting them both enough playing time just at the small forward spot."

"Good point, Cody," Coach Miller concurred. "But we'll still need a sub at the two spot, especially since both of our one-guards are pretty much pure point players."

"And we've got two good shooting guard candidates on the Maybes list," added Coach Kelley from her perch by the marker board, tapping the sec-ond line under the Maybes column.

"And don't forget the Carter girl," said Coach MacDonald. "We've got her listed as a point guard, but she played both guard positions for us last year on JV."

The assistants looked expectantly at Coach Miller. The head coach pulled her bottom lip thoughtfully as she studied the names on the board. "OK," she said finally. "Looks to me like we can probably keep two of those three guards. Carter and Smithson are both sophomores, and both played JV last year. Emma Larson's one of our two returnees on the Maybe list. She's a junior, good attitude, great defender, but a little scant on shooting for a two-guard."

Coach Kelley picked up where her boss left off. "And we were able to make use of Emma's rebounding talents at small forward some last year, although I don't suppose she'd see much action there this year now that we've got Kiefer *and* McMahon."

"Truthfully, I don't see that your extra two girl is going to see much playing time, period," commented Coach MacDonald. "Considering that, maybe we should go with Carter, since she can step in at either guard position, and Larson, since she's already proved she can handle lots of bench time and still bring a good attitude to practice."

"Yeah," agreed Coach Tyler. "Smithson probably would be better off getting another year of floor time on JV than riding the bench for the A-squad."

"Sounds good to me," said Coach Miller. "All agreed?" She scanned the others' faces. "OK, then. Randi—you can move Carter and Larson over to the Definites and Smithson to JV. That just leaves two more positions to consider—and we've already got eleven keepers."

Coach Kelley stepped in to summarize the situation. "Basically we're looking at possibly pulling one extra forward out of those three kids left at the three and four positions. We've got two juniors there: Melby, who made varsity last year but saw hardly any game time, and Doherty, who played JV as a sophomore last year. In my opinion, the freshman Olsen has actually looked more promising than either of them at tryouts, but I have to wonder if she's good enough to skip straight from the eighth-grade squad last year to varsity this year."

"And Melby's a pure three, really too small to sub in at power forward," added Coach Miller. "And we're all agreed that there won't be many spare minutes at small forward with McMahon and Kiefer covering that turf."

"Yeah," agreed her assistant. "Though it'll be tough to cut a veteran like Erin. Guess one of us two better make that phone call, eh?"

Her boss nodded. "That's going to be a real hard one. Better put her on my list."

As the varsity coaches finished conferring, the JV coaches pressed on with the work at hand. "So that cut leaves just two more to look at," noted Coach MacDonald. "Katie Doherty was a decent forward for us on JV last year. She started at the four spot and has decent size at 5'10". But I don't see her having either the strength to help out at center or the shooting touch to fill in as an emergency shooting guard. That limits her effectiveness for you on varsity, I'm afraid. Plus, she'd be a returning senior next year and unlikely to make the squad again with the talent we have coming up behind her."

Coach Kelley nodded. "That's a good point, Louise. If she's not really going to help us much this year, I think we should just bite the bullet and cut her now."

"What about the freshman, Jenny Olsen?" asked Coach Tyler. "She's listed as a three but she held her own in scrimmages when we stuck her in at the four spot."

"Yeah, and she's definitely the best shooter and ballhandler of those three, and she has tons of potential. She might even grow some yet. What is she, 5'9" or so?" Coach MacDonald checked her notes and answered her own question. "Yup. She'd be a force for us on JV, but I can see how she might be a good backup for you on varsity. I also think she's got a great attitude and could learn from playing against your kids in practice, even if she had to sit for most of the games."

"But we said the same thing about Knudson, and we decided to let her spend her freshman year on JV to get more playing time," said the JV assistant. "And there are two solid players ahead of each of them at the three and five positions."

"Cody's got a good point there," said Coach Miller. "I'm almost inclined just to go with the 11 we have, and maybe move one of those two fresh-men up later in the season if either of them looks ready and we need an extra body."

Coach Kelley finished rewriting the varsity list, this time by class year. The final 11-player roster took shape on the whiteboard:

Seniors:	Juniors:	Sophomores:
Barb McMahon	Jamie Johnson	Tina Behrens
Millie Meyer	Brenda Thorson	Anna Kiefer
Mollie Meyer	Emma Larson	Kelly Carter
	Jeri Swanson	
	Bernie Luskey	

The four coaches took a final look at the list. "Look good to everybody?" asked Coach Miller. Hearing assent all around, she concluded, "Then it's on to the hardest part: delivering the news." She quickly assigned each coach a list of players. As the others left, she picked up her telephone. «

CHAPTER *THIRTEEN*

JAMIE AND BARB SAT ON THE FRONT STEP of the Johnsons' house next to a rotting pumpkin. Barb lifted the lid off the jack-o-lantern to peer inside the blackened cavity. "Think it's about time to ditch the pumpkin?" she asked.

Jamie feigned surprise at the thought. "Come on; Halloween was only a few weeks ago." She grinned as her friend gingerly set the shriveled top back on the sagging pumpkin. "We just got our first stay-on-the-ground snow this morning. What's the big hurry?"

The two girls had already swept the light dusting of snow off the driveway by the basketball hoop in preparation for a frosty Saturday game of one on one. Barb clapped her mittened hands together. "Whew! This air is cold enough to freeze your nose hairs!"

"Yeah," Jamie said as she clasped her arms around the double layer of oversized sweatshirts that she wore. "I should have remembered when it turned cold last night to bring the basketball into the house. But it should only be a little bit longer before it warms up enough to bounce again. I brought it in from the garage as soon as you called and said you were coming over." Jamie checked her wristwatch. "While we're waiting, fill me in on what Erin said when you talked to her this morning."

Barb pulled her stocking cap farther down over her ears, then gave her report in a cloud of frosty breath. "I don't think it was such a big surprise to her, getting the 'cut' call last night. She and Emma were both worried from day one, and she knows she was just in the tougher position as far as what the team needed this year. She said she felt like she gave it her best shot over the summer and at tryouts, and she's not sure she would have wanted to keep working that hard just to sit the bench anyway."

"You said she's passing up playing on the JV team?" asked Jamie.

"Yup. I can't really blame her," said Barb. "Not after playing varsity last year. Plus she wants to spend the extra time on her reporting job at the school paper. She's gunning to be sports editor of the *Thunderbird Press* next year, she said."

"Just think of the coverage our team will get!" exclaimed Jamie. She shuffled her feet in the film of snow on the doorstep. "Amy called me while you were on your way over. She sounded a little bummed."

"I figured she would be," replied Barb, "but she'll probably be the first one they bring up from JV if we need an extra player."

"Yeah, she sounded pretty determined to earn her way up by playoffs. And I told her the playing time on JV would really help her. Coach MacDonald played center in college, so Amy should get some great help from her at the JV practices."

"If Amy picks up stuff from her as fast as she did from Karin during that pickup game last summer, she might be crowding Millie for a starting spot on varsity by the end of the season! Plus she's only a freshman."

Jamie nodded her head. "Yeah, and none of the freshmen made the cut this year. But I'll bet Jenny could make it up to varsity by the end, too, especially if your tired old legs give out by the end of the season."

Barb rolled her eyes, then grabbed Jamie's wrist for a look at her watch. "Hey, you think that ball's warmed up yet?"

Just then the front door opened a crack. "Here," said Jason. "The Universal Gas Law has worked its magic." A small bare hand thrust a basketball out through the narrow opening. The boy dropped the ball on the cement step and watched as it rolled down the steps past the bundled-up girls. "By the time it freezes up again, you'll have frostbite anyway."

"Thanks, Mr. Wizard," Jamie called after the retreating figure as the door slammed shut. She stood up and peeled off her gloves, then picked up the rejuvenated basketball. "Guess we better get to work if I'm going to have you ready to beat out Kiefer for your starting spot in two weeks. Ready to go at it, Ace?" she challenged Barb.

"You betcha!" replied her friend, yanking off her mittens. "Prepare to be smoked!" «

CHAPTER *FOURTEEN*

"SOUNDS A LITTLE DIFFERENT in here today, eh?" Millie dribbled her ball over to the side basket where Anna and Jamie were taking turns launching warm-up shots.

Jamie threw a glance at the folding divider that now ran down the middle of the gym. Muffled sounds of voices and bouncing balls from the JV squad filtered through the seams of the thin panels. "Seems weird to just have 11 of us in here today, and only half the gym," replied Jamie, "especially after all those weeks with almost 30 of us shooting around together."

A faint whistle sounded beyond the divider. Anna cocked her head, then looked around to make sure their two coaches were still huddled over their clipboards on the sideline. "Guess the JV-ers are starting their stretching," she noted. "S'pose we ought to round up the troops and get started, too?"

Millie laughed and shook her finger at the newcomer. "You trying to take over my job?" she demanded with mock concern.

"Well, hey," interjected Jamie, "if you seniors won't step up, *somebody* has to remind the coaches it's the first day of real practice."

Millie stuck out her tongue at the sassy point guard, then jogged over to the coaches. A moment later a whistle shrilled. The players loped over to toss their balls in the big wire bin at the sideline before gathering at center court for stretching.

A few minutes later, the players were taking their traditional trot around the gym. As they were finishing the second lap, Coach Miller beckoned them over toward the scorer's table. "Sorry to sit you down now that you're all limbered up," she began, "but I have a couple things to say before we get into our drills for the day."

The players plopped down on the floor around the two coaches. The head coach handed her clipboard over to her assistant, then leaned back against the table and crossed her arms. She looked around the loose circle of earnest faces. "This is it!" she began. "Today we start a new season. After the success we had last year, expectations are high: mine, yours, your families' and friends', the school's—heck, the whole town's!"

Murmurs of approval and agreement rippled through the seated group. The coach pushed away from the table to stand upright, putting her hands on her hips and narrowing her eyes. *"But,"* she cautioned, "this is a new year and a new team, and the work starts all over again. High expectations mean more pressure, more attention. This year we won't be taking anybody by surprise. You can bet that other coaches, other teams, are already circling the dates of their games with us on their calendars."

She put her hands in her pockets and paced briskly in front of the group.

Coming to a halt, she clasped her hands behind her back and looked intently into the players' eyes. "We all know what our main goal is this year," she reminded them. "It won't satisfy any of us just to win districts this year. Nope, this time we want to take the next step and win the regional championship." Claps and yells erupted from the circle of seated players.

"Remember the feeling in that huddle after that last game in March?" asked the coach. "When you promised these three," she gestured to the senior captains seated at her feet, "that you'd get them to the state tournament their senior year?"

Heads bobbed as the coach reached to pick up a folded sheet of yellow paper from a pile on the scorer's table behind her. "We don't have much time to prepare for our first game," she said, consulting the schedule sheet. "Today's Monday, the twenty-second of November, and our first game is just two weeks from tomorrow."

"We do have two new players this year," the coach continued, nodding to Anna and Kelly, "but you've all been working together since the beginning of captains' practices in September. We'll be trying out some different lineups, especially in the early games. That means everybody has to be willing to make some sacrifices, be it sitting on the bench, playing out of position, or whatever needs to be done for the good of the team."

The upturned faces looked more somber now, and some restlessness showed in the quiet shifting of arms and shuffling of feet. The head coach paused till the rustling subsided, then waved the schedule sheet in the air once more. "I want you all to remember that it's a long season ahead—a *very* long season. We start out with a pair of nonconference games, then we head into the league schedule. Home and away with each of the nine other conference teams means 18 league games, plus one more nonconference game mixed in later on. I pulled some strings and managed to schedule last year's state champions in our class to play us at the Shelby College gym in January."

"Cool!" "Excellent!" "We'll show 'em, Coach!" Cheers and handclaps punctuated the exclamations.

Coach Miller smiled, then held up a hand to quiet the uproar. "Those of you who played on this team last year know that the game schedule for regionals is brutal—three games in five days. And the next week it's the same thing all over again at the state tournament. That's where all of that conditioning you did last summer will really pay off. But the playoffs are a long time away. We have to play the season one game at a time, accomplish one goal at a time. First, we have to win the conference, and you all know there are some tough teams to beat there. Then the two conference champs in our district play off for the district title. All that, just to get *into* regionals.

"As I said, we have some big challenges to face. But if you will just trust our decisions, and each other, I have full confidence that we can get our seniors into the state tournament, and fulfill that promise you made to them last spring." More cheers broke loose.

Coach Miller interrupted the celebration, cautioning the players, "Just remember, one game at a time. Our immediate goal is to be ready for St. Mary's Academy two weeks from tomorrow." The coach stopped her pacing and glanced at her watch. "And we better get busy doing just that!" she concluded. "Let's pull in together for a quick huddle, then take two more laps to get the kinks out of those legs before we start the first drill."

The players rose eagerly from their cross-legged perches and crowded in around the coaches. "On three, *team!*" commanded Captain Barb, placing her palm on top of the stack of hands. The hands bounced in rhythm to her cadence. *"One, two, three, TEAM!"* thundered the players. The huddle broke, and the 11 girls galloped off for their two circuits of the court. ⊰

CHAPTER *FIFTEEN*

JAMIE JOGGED IN PLACE ON THE SIDELINE, nervous hands fluttering at her sides as the announcer finished introducing the visiting St. Mary's lineup. Finally the amplified voice intoned, *"And now, for the Torrington Thunderbirds, starting at guard, a junior, Number 11, Jamie Johnson!"* The roar of the home crowd gave Jamie goose bumps as she ran out to center court. She tried to stifle her anxious dance as she awaited the arrival of her fellow starters.

"Also at guard, a sophomore, Number 15, Bettina Behrens!" Jamie reached her hands up and out to smack palms with Tina as she trotted out onto the court.

"This is it, Teenie!" Jamie yelled into Tina's ear.

"Yeah. Finally!" responded Tina, giving her backcourt mate a quick hug.

"At forward, Number 22, a senior and co-captain, Barbara McMahon!"

Barb sprinted out to join the two guards. More hand slaps. The introduction of the twins completed their lineup. The crowd noise crescendoed as the rest of the team ran out to join the five starters for a quick cheer.

As the team jogged back over to the sideline, the roar finally faded enough to let the announcer introduce the Torrington coaching staff. The playing of the national anthem further quieted the crowd before the noise peaked again as the final notes faded. The coaches pulled the team in close for a few last words of advice. "Remember our game plan, now," Coach Miller shouted over the din. "Check your matchups when you line up for the center jump. If we win the toss, I want you to push the ball up the court, quick passes, just like in practice."

Coach Kelley took her turn. "On defense, we drop back into a half-court player-to-player. If you're on the ballhandler, play aggressive nose-to-the-ball and fight through any screens. One pass away, deny the passing lane. Two passes away, sag in toward the basket to help. Call out screens. Call out shots. Be vocal; communicate. Be ready to block out hard. They're a big, physical team, but we should be able to out-quick them if we keep our heads in the game."

The head coach stepped back in as the ref sounded her whistle. "Hands!" she commanded. As the players piled their palms excitedly on hers, the coach nodded to Millie.

The big center called out, "On three, *teamwork!*" A count, a shout, and the huddle broke open. The starting five took their places for the jump.

As Millie crouched to contest the toss, Jamie backpedaled a few steps toward the Saints' basket. Tina stayed up on the circle, eyeing the ball and the opposing guards. Mollie and Barb toed the circle on the opposite side, facing Millie and jockeying for position with their defenders.

Millie noticed that Mollie had her St. Mary's counterpart pinned on her hip toward the outside of the court. A glance passed between the sisters; up went the toss, up went the jumpers, and out flicked the ball, right toward Mollie's outstretched hand.

The big forward snagged the ball, then pivoted to look down the court. There was Barb, racing down the sideline to her left. Mollie hit Barb smartly in the hands with an overhead pass, then broke opposite her pass to set a quick screen for Tina. Barb pulled up and eyed the basket, setting herself for the 15-foot shot. As the Saints defender stepped up to stop her, Barb led Tina with a perfect bounce pass. Layup. Good. 2–0, Torrington.

Jamie brushed Barb's outstretched fingers with her own as they hustled back down the court. "Just like practice!" Jamie shouted. Barb grinned and gave her a quick thumbs-up.

Jamie picked up the Saints dribbler just as she crossed half court. Jamie poured all her nervous energy into her defense: knees bent, arms at the ready, head even with the ball, eyes on her opponent's waistband. Her opponent hesitated, pulling up but keeping her dribble, searching for an open teammate. In flicked Jamie's hand; out popped the ball.

Jamie scrambled after the ball, but Tina beat her to it. The crowd roared as Tina flew toward the Torrington basket, almost drowning out the shriek of the late whistle.

"*Foul, Number 11 gold, reaching in!*" The ref held up her left hand, pointing at Jamie with her right. A massive groan swept the stands.

"No sweat, Jamers," said Barb. "Way to be aggressive."

Tina jogged past, flipping the ball to the ref on the sideline. "Yeah, Jamie—keep after 'em hard like that. We'll get 'em on the next one!"

The Saints center inbounded the ball against the Thunderbirds zone.

Two quick passes, another deflection, this time by Millie in the middle. The tipped ball caromed toward the baseline, just barely eluding Mollie's one-handed reach. The basketball fell into the arms of a surprised St. Mary's forward. She pivoted toward the middle, hooking the ball up softly over the front of the rim as Mollie scrambled to recover. Swish. Another whistle. *"On the arm, gold 54. Basket's good. One shot."*

Mollie scowled as she raised her hand to acknowledge the foul. As she took her place along the lane line, she muttered to herself, "Two hands, Meyer! Grab the ball with two hands!"

The Saints forward drained the free throw. St. Mary's had their first lead at 3–2. Not for long, though. Barb lofted a three pointer on the next possession. Nothing but net. 5–3, Torrington.

By the end of the first quarter, the Thunderbirds had built an eight-point cushion. During the brief break, Coach Miller congratulated the team on their strong start, then cautioned them, "Watch those fouls, gang. We've got five already. Two more and they're in the bonus the rest of the half. That could get us in trouble pretty fast, especially if they start hitting more of their free throws." She turned to confer with her assistant, then announced, "Okay, let's bring in some fresh legs. Anna, you're in for Barb. Bernie in for Millie. On three, *defense!*"

The Thunderbirds cruised through three more quarters. At game's end the scoreboard read Torrington 63, St. Mary's 48.

Coach Miller quieted the jubilant locker room with a commanding shout of "listen up!" The post-game celebration gradually subsided as the girls found seats on the bolted-down benches lining the rows of gray metal lockers. The head coach cleared her throat, then announced, "OK, good game, folks. We looked a little ragged at times, and we committed *way* too many fouls, but for a first game, I'll take it."

Coach Kelley stepped up, clipboard in hand. "One thing to think about before practice tomorrow: we need to work harder on making contact on our blockouts when a shot goes up. They got too many offensive rebounds—*nine* of them. That's just lack of concentration, girls. If we don't get that fixed by Friday, Minneapolis Central will clean our clocks."

Eleven heads turned as Coach Miller stepped up again. "I promise not to keep you from the showers too long here. I just want to remind you that we only have two more days of practice before we take on a little bigger challenge than St. Mary's gave us tonight. As you all know, Central is a bigger school, Class AA, and a very competitive program. Should be a good test for us, and I think we'll be ready for it." She stepped back and glanced down at her seated captains. "Any comments to add?" she asked the three seniors.

Millie and Mollie exchanged glances, then deferred to Barb. The forward got to her feet. "Nice job tonight, T-birds—way to start us on the road to the playoffs!" she said. Whistles and cheers erupted in answer, drawing the other two co-captains to their feet.

"Pull in here together, everybody," yelled Millie, as Mollie waved their teammates in toward the middle of the crowded aisle. "Last cheer of the night: on three, *keep it up!*"

As the huddle broke up, Coach Kelley shouted over the cheers. "I want all those towels and uniforms off the floor and in the laundry bin before you leave!" «

CHAPTER SIXTEEN

T-Birds Fall Just Short, Central Steals Win
Newcomer shines for Torrington as Class AA contenders get scare

By Erin Melby
The Thunderbird Press

MINNEAPOLIS — The Central High Vikings walked away with a victory, but it was not exactly a walk in the park.

Central came out blazing, their big guns staking the Vikings to a 19–7 lead in the first quarter of play. Enter Anna Kiefer, Torrington's import from Iowa.

"Kiefer really lit a fire under us," said Thunderbird coach Sharon Miller. "She wasn't the least bit intimidated by their big-city reputation."

The sophomore forward's scrappy defense led to three second-quarter steals, which the Thunderbirds converted into layups. The inside tandem of Millie and Mollie Meyer then kicked into gear, blocking shots and snatching offensive boards from the bigger Vikings front line.

By halftime, the Class A underdogs had dug out of their opening period hole. The stunned Vikings trailed 38–37 going into the break.

"We got lazy when we built that big early lead," speculated Central coach Martin Rosenberg. "I warned my girls before the game that we couldn't take this team lightly."

Torrington opened the third quarter with a pair of threes by Kiefer and point guard Jamie Johnson. The seven-point lead and a Rosenberg timeout tirade finally reawakened the groggy Vikings defense. Central chipped away at the T-bird lead, pulling even at 54–all as the third quarter ticked to a close.

The final period was a back-and-forth battle, with the lead changing hands seven times. The play that sealed Torrington's fate may have been the fifth foul on Thunderbird guard Tina

Behrens with just under a minute remaining and the Vikings up by two.

With Behrens on the bench, Kiefer rotated over to shooting guard and senior Barbara McMahon returned at forward. The Vikes converted both ends of the one-and-one. A Thunderbird timeout set up a backdoor layup off the ensuing full-court press, but a foul by McMahon put Central back on the line. The resulting pair of free throws gave Central their final margin of 69–65.

Monday at noon the lunch crowd was huddled over a copy of the school newspaper spread across the team table. "Looks like Erin gave us a pretty good write-up!" said Jeri.

"Yeah." said Jamie, "but she made it sound like Barb lost us the game there at the end with that foul."

Behind Jamie's shoulder, Barb was shaking her head. "She just told it like it was, Jamie."

Jamie whipped around, eyes flashing indignantly. "You were just doing what the coaches called for. It's not like we had any choice. Down by two, and they had the ball. We didn't have time to let them walk it up the court!"

Millie chimed in, "Yeah, Barb, you did exactly what the coaches diagrammed in that last timeout: get the quick layup, then foul to get the ball back."

Anna had been standing silently on the edge of the gathering. She glanced at Barb, then quietly added, "It's not like you weren't going for the ball. They did call it a one-and-one, not a flagrant foul, which would have given them two shots—and the ball."

Again Barb shook her head. "But I waited too long. There were five seconds left when they inbounded the ball and less than a second left by the time I managed to foul my girl. Not to mention that she was their best foul shooter, instead of that sub Coach Kelley told us to target."

"Come on, don't be a martyr," said Jamie. "You waited four seconds because they got the inbound pass to the good shooter instead of the sub." Jamie turned to throw a challenging look over her shoulder. "Right, Anna?"

Recalling her role as defender of the poor-shooting sub, Anna nodded ruefully. "I wasn't thinking," she admitted. "If I hadn't guarded my girl so close, maybe they'd have passed it to her. Then I could have fouled her instead."

"Yeah, and been an even bigger hero," growled Jamie under her breath.

Barb looked sharply at her scowling friend. The captain sensed a crisis brewing. "I think we should focus on the fact that we almost knocked off one of the best teams in the state," she urged, "not argue about something that's history now anyway." She picked up the newspaper and folded in it half. Turning to face Anna, she said, "Without you in there, we'd've never even had the chance to be playing for the win there at the end." She handed Anna the paper. "Here—I'll bet your mom might like an extra copy of the paper to send to your relatives back in Iowa."

Anna smiled gratefully, accepting the peace offering. Just then the bell sounded, signaling the end of the lunch period. Anna looked relieved to be spared coming up with a fitting response. "See you all at practice, then," she blurted as the group began to scatter.

Barb called after the retreating heads, "Fire up, troops! One more day till our first league game!" «

CHAPTER *SEVENTEEN*

THE THUNDERBIRDS HAD WON THEIR FIRST FOUR league games, but Jamie just didn't feel right about how Anna was affecting the team chemistry. It would be good to have a little break over the holidays.

Two days before Christmas, Jamie rolled reluctantly out of her warm bed as the smell of frying bacon wafted up to her room. She grabbed a fuzzy fleece bathrobe off the floor. Wrapping the red robe over her rumpled T-shirt, she shuffled down the stairs and into the kitchen.

Jamie mumbled a "good morning" to her mother, who was forking sizzling strips of bacon onto a plate lined with paper towels. After a stretch and a yawn, Jamie snitched a piece of bacon as her mother bent to put the platter into the warm oven.

Mrs. McMahon reached for a carton of eggs and began cracking them into a bowl. "What time are you and Barb getting together tomorrow?"

she asked. The two girls had a years-long tradition of meeting on the afternoon of Christmas Eve to exchange presents.

"Uh ... I'm not sure," Jamie replied as she delicately nibbled the edges of the hot bacon strip. "Barb invited Anna to stay with them over the holidays so she wouldn't have to miss practice." At her mother's puzzled look, Jamie explained, "Anna's family left today to spend Christmas with relatives back in Iowa, and they won't be back for a week."

"And your plans for tomorrow?" prompted her mother.

Irritated, Jamie shoved the rest of the piece of bacon into her mouth, pausing to chew and swallow before she replied. "Guess I'll just talk to Barb at practice today and see if she still wants to do it."

"Well, of course she will! It's your tradition," said Mrs. Johnson. As she poured the beaten eggs into the hot frying pan she added, "And how kind of the McMahons to take Anna in with them like that."

"No kidding," interjected Jason from his seat at the kitchen table where he'd been quietly reading the morning paper. "Especially since Anna's looking like she might push Barb out of her starting job any day now." He pushed his glasses up on his nose without raising his eyes from the newspaper. If he'd seen his sister's face, he might have kept his next comment to himself. "Up in the bleachers at last night's game I heard some kids saying she'd have lost it by now if she wasn't a senior and a captain."

"That just shows how much those idiots know!" Jamie exploded hotly. "Anna might be a flashy shooter and she might get a spectacular steal once in a while, but she can't touch Barb as an all-around team player. Anybody with a brain can see that."

"Whoa, Nellie!" cried Jason as he shielded himself with the want ads. "Are we a little defensive on this topic?"

Jamie glared at her brother. Mrs. Johnson plopped the plate of scrambled eggs down between them. "Let's calm down, please. Jason, would you get the bacon out of the oven and get the orange juice from the fridge? And Jamie, if you'd clear the paper away and set the table while I finish the toast, we'll be ready to eat."

‹‹ ‹ T › ›› ›

A few hours later, Barb was dressing for practice as Jamie entered the locker room. "Where's Anna?" asked Jamie.

"I don't know," answered Barb from her seat on the bench. "She's not coming over to our house till tonight."

"So, do you still want to get together and do the present thing tomorrow?"

"Huh? Of course!" Barb dropped her shoelace in mid-tie and looked up at Jamie. "What on earth made you think that I wouldn't?"

"Well, I just figured with Anna there and all ..."

"Well, you figured wrong, ya goofball. All that energy I spent shopping and wrapping is certainly *not* going to go to waste!" Barb aimed a punch at Jamie's arm, nearly toppling from her seat on the bench when Jamie sidestepped the blow.

Jamie laughed as she reached out a hand to steady her falling friend. "Okay, okay ... How about I'll see if I can get Mom's car and pick you up around 2:00? We can cruise up to the park or something. Get away from the family festivities for a little while."

"Sounds good," agreed Barb. "I'll need to be back by 5:00 at the latest, for the dinner-and-presents routine."

"Hey, Johnson!" boomed a voice from the far end of the row of lockers.

"Hey, Luskey!" replied Jamie, flinging a stray wad of athletic tape in the direction of Bernie.

"Can you give me a hand with this combination?" the big center banged the padlock on her locker in disgust.

"Guess you better go rescue Sister B," Barb said to Jamie. "I'll see you out on the floor."

‹‹ ‹‹ ‹‹ 𝕋 ›› ›› ››

The township park was blanketed with a fresh covering of Christmas Eve snow. Two well-bundled figures trudged through the drifts toward the old metal swing set at the far side of the park.

Barb reached the swings first. She grabbed a pair of chains in her mittened hands. As Jamie watched curiously, Barb dug a seat out of the snow, then eyed the bar up high overhead. "If we throw the chains up and over that crossbar a few times, I'll bet we could get them clear enough of the snow to be able to swing."

"Whoever gets theirs up first gets to open their present first," declared Jamie, setting off a furious race of digging and flinging. A few minutes later, the snow-covered pair stood panting, two swings hanging crookedly before them, chains twisted and seats still grazing the churned pile of snow below.

"Well, maybe we're too old for swings," offered Jamie.

"Yeah, and our butts would freeze to them in two minutes anyhow," said Barb.

"How about the picnic shelter?" suggested Jamie. "We could tunnel under that stack of picnic tables. I bet there's a hollow space underneath."

"Too old for swings, but not for snow forts, eh?" chuckled Barb.

"Last one to the shelter's a Hunterville Tiger!" yelled Jamie as she took off across the park.

A half hour of digging later, the two girls sat snugly in their little igloo. "So, where's my present?" Jamie asked brightly.

"In my pocket," answered Barb, patting the side of her bulky winter coat. "But I think I should open mine first, to give you a chance to work on your patience."

Jamie unzipped her heavy parka, extracting a small box from an inside pocket. She held the package up in the dim light of their snow cave, showing off the gold foil wrapping and curled blue ribbon. "Wrapped it myself!" she announced proudly. She presented the box to Barb with a flourish.

Barb held out her mittened palm to accept the little package. She eyed it from all sides, finally commenting, "I'm impressed! All these years I've known you, and still you surprise me with untold talents."

"Go on, open it," urged Jamie.

"Okay, okay, hold your horses," laughed Barb as she pulled off her mittens. "I hate to ruin this elegant wrap job."

"Just rip it!" ordered Jamie.

Barb finally yanked off the ribbon and tore open the shiny wrapping to reveal a small cardboard box. She pried open the flap at one end, pulling out a wad of green tissue paper. She peered into the box, then turned it upside down and shook it. "Empty!" she proclaimed.

"It's in the paper, Doughbrain." Jamie pointed to the crumpled wad in Barb's lap.

Barb grinned, knowing well her old friend's impatience when it came to opening presents. She carefully and deliberately unrolled the layers of tissue, finally revealing a light green ceramic tube with tapered ends. It had a dark green blob with a stem at one end and a pair of thin metal rings around the middle. "Okay, I give. What is it?" she asked Jamie.

"Turn it over," instructed Jamie.

Barb did so, revealing a line of words inscribed in black on the glossy green surface, interrupted halfway by the metal rings. "*Two peas … in a pod*," she read out loud.

"Open it," ordered Jamie, miming a bending motion with her hands.

Barb found the hinge on the little enameled box and bent the two ends back to snap it open. Out tumbled two tiny green glass peas, each bearing pink cheeks and a smiling face.

"I thought you might need something to keep on your desk in the dorm room next year to remind you not to forget your best friend back home," explained Jamie.

Barb rolled the little peas around in her hand, touched by her friend's sentiment. "It's perfect. Here," she said impulsively, dropping one of the little glass spheres into Jamie's hand. "You keep this one on *your* desk at home. Maybe it'll bring you some luck when you need it next basketball season when I'm not around to tell you what to do."

Jamie rolled her eyes. "I doubt you could get far enough away to keep you from doing that." She tucked the smiling pea into a little zippered compartment on the back of her mitten. "Speaking of which, any more news from the colleges you're thinking about applying to?"

"Well, my sister Colleen's going to let me stay with her up at the U for a night after Christmas break so I can go to a few classes and talk to some of the engineering profs."

"That'd be cool, if you ended up in Minneapolis, just an hour and a half away," said Jamie. "But what about basketball?"

Barb idly rattled the remaining pea in the ceramic pod. "Yeah, going to a Big Ten school probably would mean the end of my basketball career, except maybe intramurals. I don't think I'd have a chance to even make it as a walk-on at Minnesota."

"You heard from any other places, any smaller colleges where you could do the engineering stuff and still play basketball?"

"Yeah, a couple. But they're all pretty far away."

"Like where?"

"Well, one's in Virginia. One's in Boston. One's in Pennsylvania. All over the place."

"Jeez," said Jamie. "I didn't realize you were looking anywhere that far away." She stared out the door of the snow tunnel, then brightened at the thought of her present yet to be opened. "Okay, my turn," she said, holding out her hand.

Barb reached into her coat pocket. Slowly she withdrew a flat, oblong box. She held the package tantalizingly high before finally dropping it into Jamie's waiting palm. "I see we both went for the school color scheme," Barb commented as Jamie eyed the blue wrapping and gold stick-on bow.

Jamie was already busy pulling off the bow and stripping the paper from the box. She flipped off the cover, then lifted a thin layer of white cotton batting. Underneath lay a golden figure of a fierce-looking bird with red-jeweled eyes and lightning forking from its talons. Jamie lifted the medallion by its thin gold chain, holding it up so the dim winter light caught the eyes and made them gleam.

"A Thunderbird, of course," said Barb.

"It's beautiful," said Jamie.

Barb reached out to touch the golden figure dangling from its chain. "You know, there's quite a legend behind the Thunderbirds."

"Oh yeah?" said Jamie as she lowered the gleaming figure carefully back into its nest of cotton.

Barb clasped her hands around her knees. "Native American tribes considered the Thunderbird a guardian spirit," she said, gazing out the door of their little shelter. "According to the ancient stories, he was a huge bird, as long as two canoes, with feathers as long as paddles. His eyes flashed lightning, they said, and his wings produced thunder."

"Sounds more like an *evil* spirit to me" scoffed Jamie. "Say, where did you learn all this legend stuff?"

"Well, I showed the necklace to Anna this morning," Barb admitted. "She was hanging around my room when I was wrapping it. Apparently her grandma's a Chippewa Indian, and she'd tell Anna all these old stories and stuff."

Annoyed that Anna had seen her present, Jamie glanced at her watch and changed the subject. "Hey, it's quarter to five. Don't you have to be back home by five?"

"Yikes!" exclaimed Barb, stuffing her gift in a pocket and pulling her mittens back on. "I'm glad you noticed the time. Little Rosie'll kill me if I make her wait one minute longer than necessary to start opening presents at home. She's almost as bad as you are." ◄

CHAPTER EIGHTEEN

Torrington to Play Defending State Champs
7–1 Thunderbirds face second big challenge in game at Shelby College

By Erin Melby
The Thunderbird Press

TORRINGTON — The Torrington Thunderbirds have rattled off six straight wins to start their league schedule this season, but the bar will be raised when they face defending Class A champion Coleman in tomorrow night's non-conference contest at Shelby College.

Coleman enters the game undefeated at 8–0 and again ranked #1 in the latest Class A state poll. Torrington's perfect 6–0 conference tally and close loss to Class AA power Minneapolis Central have vaulted the Thunderbirds to a #9 ranking, their first Top 10 rating ever.

"This is a perfect test for us at this point in the season," said Torrington coach Sharon Miller. "We match up against Coleman pretty well, but we know they'll give us a stiff challenge."

The surprise of the season for Torrington has been the play of sophomore forward Anna Kiefer. The transplanted Iowan has sparked the Thunderbirds with stellar play off the bench, averaging 16 points a game while splitting time at the small forward position with senior co-captain Barbara McMahon.

"McMahon's our team leader and one of our steadiest players," said Coach Miller, "but Kiefer gives us a definite boost whether we need some quick hands on defense or a three-point threat on offense."

Torrington's front court twins Millie and Mollie Meyer have also been lighting up the scoreboard, averaging a combined five blocked shots, 18 rebounds, and 25 points on the season.

Rounding out the Thunderbird assault are guards Tina Behrens and Jamie Johnson, respective team leaders in steals and assists.

Miller warned against putting too much emphasis on the outcome of Friday's contest, noting that entry into the district playoffs depends only on the conference record. Of the 10 Valley Conference teams, only Torrington and Mason remain undefeated, promising an exciting showdown January 25 on the Bobcats' home floor.

Jamie tapped her foot impatiently as Mrs. Morgan stretched her last-period history class a few seconds beyond the bell. As soon as the teacher ended her lecture, Jamie rocketed out the door and made a beeline for the locker room. She burst through the door already shedding clothes, stopping short at the sight of Barb and Anna side by side on the taping table, engrossed in Thursday's edition of the Thunderbird Press.

"What does our star reporter have to say about us today?" asked Jamie.

Barb was startled at the sound of Jamie's voice. "Not a whole lot," she answered. "They gave her extra space yesterday for that big article she wrote about our win over Carson City Tuesday night, but she did manage two columns on the front page today."

Anna retreated toward her locker as Jamie reached for the paper. "I have to go to a captains' meeting," said Barb, avoiding Jamie's eyes. "I'll see you out on the floor."

Jamie waved absently, engrossed in her reading. Two minutes later she was crumpling up the newspaper. "Hmmph!" she snorted, flinging the wadded paper into the trash. She looked up in time to see Anna disappearing through the door out onto the court. «

CHAPTER NINETEEN

FRIDAY NIGHT THE SHELBY GYM WAS PACKED. The south bleachers overflowed with blue and gold, the north side with Coleman green and white. Jamie stood stone-faced on the sideline as the Commodores' starting lineup was announced. She shook her head as if to clear it, then stared up at the scoreboard suspended above the middle of the court. She hardly noticed the green uniforms gathering at center court, barely heard the introductions or the response of the Coleman fans.

"And now, the starting lineup for the Torrington Thunderbirds!"

A roar of applause swelled, drowning out the announcer. When the din finally receded, the amplified voice continued, *"At guard, Number 11, Jamiieeee e... JOHNSON!"* Jamie pulled her focus back to the court. She jogged out to the center circle, where she stood rigidly, hands on hips.

"Also at guard, Number 15, Bettinaaaaa ... BEHRENS!" Tina trotted

out to join Jamie for the usual hand smack.

"Come on, Johnson," entreated Tina. "Fire up!"

"Huh? Oh, yeah ..." replied Jamie, looking down at her hightops.

"*At forward,*" the announcer boomed, "*Number 32, Annaaaa ... KIEFER!*"

Standing on the sideline, Barb gave Anna a slap on the back to shove her out onto the court. "Go get 'em, Anna!" she hollered.

Anna reached center court, reaching up high to slap Tina's waiting palms. Jamie held her hands out, grimly accepting Anna's tentative tap.

Anna took her place next to Tina as the announcer introduced Mollie. The big forward rambled out onto the court, waving to acknowledge the explosion of cheers from the south stands. She exchanged hand slaps with Anna, then Tina. When she came to Jamie, she grabbed the point guard's outstretched hands and pulled her closer. "Come on, Johnson, get over it!" Mollie whispered fiercely in Jamie's ear. "We've got a game to play here!"

Jamie stared across the floor to where Barb stood clapping as Millie's name was being called. "I can't believe this," Jamie seethed. "And you two were in on it, too. That captains' meeting yesterday. She didn't even have the guts to tell me herself."

Mollie gave Jamie a warning look as Millie approached the line of players. The twins gathered the starting five for the usual cheer before leading them back to the bench.

Coach Miller bent into the huddle, straining to be heard over the crowd noise. "Listen up, now! This is where we see if we deserve that Top 10 ranking. I'm expecting them to come out in a full-court press, so be ready. Quick passes—keep the ball in the middle of the court. If we don't dribble into a corner trap, we should be fine."

As the head coach straightened up, 11 faces turned to her assistant. "Remember now, help defense is a key tonight," Coach Kelley reminded them. "We know they're quick, and if we're going to stick with them player-to-player it's got to be a team effort."

The head coach glanced over at the scorer's table, where the refs were getting ready to call the teams onto the court. The coach nodded to Barb, who was standing beside her.

The captain spoke up on cue. "This is our chance to show what we're made of," she said. "All for one and one for all." Barb stuck out her hand, trying to catch Jamie's eye as the palms piled onto the stack. No dice. Barb took a deep breath. "On three, *together!*" she yelled. Barb continued to look at Jamie as she chanted the count, but Jamie just mechanically completed the cheer, then turned to run onto the court.

A crooked toss by the ref gave the Coleman center an easy tip back to her waiting teammate. As the other players streamed down toward the Commodores' basket, Jamie waited at half court to pick up the dribbler. Crouching low, Jamie smacked the floorboards with both hands. Her distant look of moments ago was replaced by a fierce scowl directed at her Coleman counterpart.

The green-jerseyed guard stood dribbling the ball with her left hand as she surveyed the court. Finally she began to advance, holding her right hand up over her head, one finger raised. Jamie lunged toward the ball just as it came up off the floor. The Coleman guard executed a quick crossover dribble and exploded past Jamie.

"Help!" yelled Jamie, backpedaling.

"Got you covered!" called Tina as she stepped forward to cut off the dribbler's path for an instant until Jamie could recover. Tina's girl took advantage of her defender's momentary move with a hard cut to the basket. Jamie's player instantly picked up her dribble and feathered a lob pass up and over the two Torrington guards. The Coleman cutter gathered in the ball just as she crashed into Anna, who had slid over to help.

A whistle sounded as gold- and green-shirted players pulled their two fallen comrades up off the floor. "Offensive foul, green 22!" barked the referee.

Mollie finished hauling Anna to her feet. "Way to take the charge, Kiefer!" the center exclaimed.

Anna brushed herself off, nodding her thanks as she stepped out of bounds to take the ball from the official. "Watch for the press!" yelled Anna as she prepared to inbound the ball.

Jamie stood directly behind Tina at the free throw line, both of them facing Anna on the endline. Anna slapped the ball once, sending the two guards in opposite directions. A fake to Jamie, then a bounce pass in to Tina. She pivoted immediately to look up the court.

Mollie stood at half court, defended loosely by the huge Commodore player behind her. Tina whipped a hard chest pass to Mollie, who shielded the ball with her elbows out as she pivoted to look toward her basket. Out of the corner of her eye, Mollie saw Jamie sprinting up the sideline to her left. Mollie knew Tina would be coming just as hard on the opposite side. She faked a lead pass to one side, then the other. The two guards continued down to the baseline, crossing under the basket and drawing their defenders with them. In Jamie's wake came Anna, wide open out on the wing.

Mollie led the trailer with a soft pass. Anna caught the ball in stride, pumped down one hard dribble, then pulled up for a long jumper just outside the arc. *Good!* 3–0, Thunderbirds.

"Nice shot, Anna!" shrieked Mollie over the roar of the crowd.

"Thanks! Nice pass!" answered Anna as she loped down the court.

"No time to celebrate yet—let's play some defense," scolded Jamie as she sprinted by.

The Commodores pushed the ball up the court. They probed the Thunderbird defense with 15 seconds of crisp passing, screening and cutting without freeing anyone for a shot. Finally Tina's player stood with the ball on the right wing and waved for a clear-out. As her teammates shifted out of the lane, the Coleman two-guard jab-stepped to Tina's left, then burst past her on the opposite side. As she drove into the lane, Jamie scrambled over to block her path. The savvy Commodore bounced a pass right into the hands of Jamie's now-open player. Layup. Good. 3–2, Torrington.

Anna stepped across the endline. As she picked up the ball, she felt a hand jostle her elbow. "Hey," growled Jamie. "You're supposed to give some help when I drop off to stop that drive."

Anna opened her mouth, then shut it again. Finally she replied quietly, "No problem, Jamie. I'll have you covered next time."

The Coleman defenders were fronting the Thunderbirds this time on the press. Their oversize center set up facing Anna at the endline, frantically flailing her long arms to block the inbounder's view of the court. Anna slapped the ball, then rapidly shuffled three steps to her left, stepped back from the endline, and heaved a long baseball pass.

At the slap of the ball, Tina had broken away down the court, leaving her defender trailing behind. Tina gathered in Anna's perfect lead pass and sped toward the basket. One defender remained. The tall Coleman forward faked a move toward Tina, then dropped back into the lane to cut off the passing lane to Millie at the low post.

As soon as the big Commodore retreated, Tina pushed on toward the basket. Her left-handed layup hit the backboard hard, then skimmed off the rim on the opposite side. Millie spun around in front of the upright defender and leaped up for the carom. At the peak of her jump, the ball touched the fingertips of her outstretched right hand. She shoved the basketball back up onto the glass as she held off the Coleman defender with her left arm.

"Basket's good, and one!" announced the ref. The south stands erupted in a prolonged clamor as Millie stepped to the free throw line.

"Way to hold your ground, Mill!" exclaimed Jamie as she trotted up to clap her center on the shoulder.

"Thanks," said Millie, wiping her hands on the back of her shorts. Just before the ref handed Millie the ball, another whistle sounded. "Timeout, green," intoned the official. Just over a minute had ticked off the game clock. The scoreboard read Torrington 5, Coleman 2.

The Thunderbirds ran over to the bench as their jubilant teammates leaped off the bench to meet them. "Great start, gang!" cheered Barb as the starters neared the sideline. "No letting up now."

The coaches pulled the huddle together to quickly announce a switch to a two-three zone defense. "They're getting by us on too many drives already," noted Coach Kelley. "So far we've been lucky that they've just gotten one layup off of it, but I want to see what we can do with the zone for a while."

Coach Miller chipped in. "Remember to find a body to box out on every shot. That'll be a little tougher out of the zone, but we *cannot* leave anybody unblocked. They're aggressive on the offensive boards, and we can't afford to give this team second or third shots." She motioned for the hands. "On three, *Keep it up!*"

As the huddle broke, Barb grabbed Jamie's arm. The point guard kept her gaze focused outward on the court. "Looking good, Jamie," Barb said to the back of her friend's head. Jamie shook off the hand and jogged wordlessly back onto the court.

Millie calmly sank the free throw. 6–2, Torrington. As the Thunderbirds backpedaled down the court, Mollie hollered, "Hands up, now. Make 'em work!" The five gold shirts deployed in their 2-3 zone as the Commodores brought the basketball up the court.

The Coleman point guard paused with the ball at the top of the key, sensing a change. A flick of her hand sent her left wing player cutting through the lane. Tina shadowed the cutter into the key, passing her off to Millie in the middle. When Anna escorted the cutter out the other side, the Coleman point guard yelled out, "Zone!"

The Commodores realigned their offensive set into a 2-1-2 formation with their gangly center set up at the high post. Millie stepped up from behind her, sticking a hand in front of her on the ball side. The Coleman player moved her arm against Millie's, bracing herself against the solid Thunderbird center while she called for the ball with her opposite hand. As the ball was lobbed in to the post, the other Thunderbird defenders shifted in toward the key. The center held the ball high as she pivoted to face the basket. She faked a shot, drawing the defense in even more. A green-jerseyed teammate popped out on the right baseline. The center snapped her a pass as Anna tore out toward the receiver.

"Shot!" screamed Anna. Five gold uniforms moved in concert, each finding a green one to seal away from the basket. The ball arced high. As it dropped toward the hoop, the Torrington players crouched low, spreading their feet wide and continuing to push back against the insistent shoving of the offensive players. "Eyes on the rim! Hands up!" shouted Coach Miller from the sideline.

The ball thunked on the iron, then bounced high to the opposite side. Mollie held her ground against her taller opponent. She grabbed for the ball, ferociously pulling it toward her chin and sticking her elbows out. The Commodore defender reached over Mollie's head, snatching at the ball. A whistle sounded. "Foul, 55 green. Over the back. Gold ball."

With less than two minutes remaining in the first quarter, the Coleman coach called his second timeout. Jamie glanced up at the scoreboard as she ran over to the sideline. Torrington 19, Coleman 12.

"Ready for a breather, Johnson?" asked the head coach. "That Coleman point guard's been pushing you pretty hard."

Jamie shook her head as she leaned over taking a deep breath. "No, not yet," she panted. "I can take her, Coach."

Anna raised her hand. "I could use a sub."

"Barb, you're in for Anna," directed the coach. "You know who you're guarding?"

"Yup," replied Barb as she stripped off her warm-up jacket. "Number 33. I've been watching her."

"Bernie, you're in for Millie at center," added the coach. "Let's go back to the player-to-player defense for now. We'll switch into the 2-3 zone anytime we make a free throw, just for one possession, just for a little change of pace." She turned to her assistant. "Think we should throw our own press at them?" she asked.

Coach Kelley shook her head. "No, not yet. We're doing fine with the half-court defense, so let's save it for later. Let them wear themselves down with their press. Our conditioning should pay off in the second half."

Coach Miller nodded her assent as the horn sounded. Barb led the team cheer, then took her place out on the floor.

Ninety-seven seconds later, the horn blasted to mark the end of the first quarter. The Thunderbirds had held their ground since the timeout, trading baskets with the favored Coleman squad. Torrington's lead still stood at seven, 21–14.

"Meyer and Kiefer, you're back in," ordered Coach Miller. "Nice work, Barb, Bernie. Keep your eyes open. We'll be needing you again soon out there." She turned to Brenda, saying, "Thorson, you're in for Johnson at the point."

Jamie spoke up, "Watch out for her speed, Bren. Just when you think she's gonna pull up and pass off, *zoom,* she's by you."

"Gotcha," Brenda replied.

The subs reported in at the scorer's table. Barb took a seat next to the coaches. Jamie eyed the empty seat next to Barb, then walked to the other end of the bench and sat down by Kelly. Jamie busied herself by giving Kelly some pointers on breaking the Commodore press.

At halftime, the spacious college locker room resounded with whoops and cheers. Coach Miller let the hoopla run its course while she conferred with her assistant. A few minutes later the head coach turned toward the waiting team while Coach Kelley wrote busily on the whiteboard behind her.

"*Excellent* first half!" the head coach began, clipboard in hand and eyes beaming. "Up by 12 on the top team in our class in the state!" She let the resulting applause and cheers subside before getting down to work.

"Are you satisfied yet?" she challenged her team.

"No way!" "Uh-uh!" "Are you kidding??" came the responses.

"Okay. Then here's what we have to do the rest of the way." The head coach turned to the board behind her, now covered with diagrams and lists. ≪

CHAPTER *TWENTY*

FROM HIS SEAT AT THE KITCHEN TABLE, Jason held out a folded section of newspaper as his sister stomped past pulling on a sweatshirt. "Here," he offered. "Erin got a column in the *Torrington Times* today." Jamie came to a halt long enough to snatch the town paper.

Thunderbirds Sink Commodores' Ship
New lineup scores big; Torrington beats defending champs by 10 points

By Erin Melby
For the Torrington Times

BARNESVILLE—It takes guts to tamper with success. Coach Sharon Miller gambled Torrington's six-game winning streak by shuffling her starting lineup for the first time in over a year. The result? A landmark victory over the top-ranked Class A team in the state.

Newcomer Anna Kiefer replaced senior co-captain Barbara McMahon as Torrington's starter at small forward. Kiefer responded with a breakout game, recording a team- and season-high 27 points in the 69–59 win.

"It was a tough call to make," admitted Miller. "But I knew we'd need the extra scoring tonight. I think our lineup change took Coleman by surprise. And once we got that quick lead, our defense never let them regain their balance."

The speedy sophomore tandem of Kiefer and guard Tina Behrens keyed the torrid Thunderbird defense. Kiefer drew four charges from the frustrated Coleman offense, while Behrens contributed six steals and a career-best eight rebounds.

McMahon took her demotion in stride. "Anna earned the chance," declared the veteran. "She never complained about being a sub, even though she was leading the team in scoring."

Despite her reduced role, McMahon produced eight points and five rebounds in 14 minutes of supporting play. Also seeing significant minutes off the bench were point guard Brenda Thorson and backup center Bernadette Luskey.

Thorson's strong play was crucial late in the third quarter after playmaker Jamie Johnson went to the bench with four fouls. Johnson returned with four minutes to go in the game but picked up number five on the next possession.

"We thought we finally caught a break there, getting Johnson in foul trouble," commented Coleman coach Darrell Morgan. "We didn't know they had that kind of backup at the point."

Next up for the 8–1 Thunderbirds squad is a road game against Twin Lake. The Titans currently have a solid hold on last place in the league at 0–6 (1–7 overall). Torrington then ends a four-game road stretch with a return to their home court next Friday against Valley Conference foe Winnebago (6–3, 4–2). League co-leader Mason looms the following week.

A banging sound on the back door finally broke through Jamie's concentration. An exasperated Jason got up to answer the door, but Jamie waved him off. "It's just Barb," she informed him as she headed toward the door.

"Oh. I'm outta here, then. Think I'll go do some homework," replied her brother.

Jamie yanked open the front door. Barb stepped over the threshold and held up a paper sack. "Dad made donuts this morning. The kind you like, with cinnamon and sugar."

"Come right in," said Jamie, the invitation in the words betrayed by the sarcasm in her voice.

"Thanks, I will," replied Barb as she began to remove her coat. "We need to talk."

"What's to talk about?" asked Jamie. "You got what you were aiming for. Your pal Anna is starting. We won the game. Everybody's happy."

"Not you," Barb pointed out.

"And what does that matter?" responded Jamie. "That didn't seem to enter your mind when you hatched your plot with the coaches."

"What do you mean?" challenged Barb.

Jamie gave her a disgusted look. "Oh yeah," she said. "Just try to tell me *they* came to *you* with this idea."

"Oh, please!" exclaimed Barb. "Come off it, Jamie. I did this for the good of the team."

"Hah! So you admit it!" Jamie burst out.

"You know the coaches wouldn't have forced that change on the team," Barb defended herself. "But everybody except you could see it was the best thing for the team. It's not like I quit or anything."

"Oh, that's right. I forgot—now you're the big cheerleader, the tragic martyr on the sideline."

Barb stopped in her tracks, stunned, speechless. She searched her friend's face. "What is this *really* about, Jamie?" she finally asked. "You're acting like I did this deliberately to hurt you personally."

"Hurt *me?*" asked Jamie in mock surprise. "Yeah well, I *was* kind of looking forward to playing our last season together ... *together,*" she emphasized. "You could have at least told me what you had up your sleeve before you went and pitched it to the coaches at the captains' meeting before practice last Thursday."

"You're probably right about that," admitted Barb. "I guess I was afraid you'd talk me out of it. You think it was easy making that decision?"

"That's not the point," snapped Jamie. "The point is that we've been best friends practically since birth, and you just cut me out. You cut me out of the decision. You never considered that we'd been aiming toward this season for years now, what it meant to me. All those dreams, all those plans." Jamie covered the choke in her voice with a cough. Clearing her throat, she continued. "Yeah, we won the game with Anna starting. Maybe we'd have won by 20 with you starting. You can't know. And now it's too late. No going back now."

Barb looked down at her hands, trying to find the words that would make things right again. "Jamie," she began, looking up and searching her friend's face. "I just don't know what to say."

Jamie had taken a seat on the bottom step of the stairs to the upper floor. Now she stood and folded her arms across her chest. "Yeah? Well, why don't you go ask your new best friend, Anna. I'm sure she'll be glad to help you."

Jamie whirled around and marched up the stairs. Barb started after her, then checked herself. She pulled on her coat, tugged on her boots, and reached down to pick up her mittens and the bag of donuts. She turned to let herself out the door, then paused, considering. She stepped back to the stairway, placing the donut bag carefully on the flat-topped post at the end of the railing. She shut the door quietly on her way out. «

CHAPTER TWENTY-ONE

WHEN BARB ARRIVED AT THE team locker room after school on Monday, she saw that the locker next to hers was already crammed with Jamie's school clothes and book bag. Disappointed, Barb glanced at her wristwatch. Six minutes till the start of practice.

Barb twirled the dial on her combination lock with practiced efficiency. Three minutes later she was dressed and pulling on her hightops, which she'd left on the floor outside her locker as usual. A hard lump jabbed the bottom of her foot as she tugged on the left shoe. "How'd I get a stone in my shoe in here?" she wondered. Off came the shoe. Barb turned it upside down and shook it over her hand. A small green glass pea rolled into her palm.

"What's that?" asked Anna as she walked past on her way out to the gym.

Barb quickly closed her fingers and turned away. "Uh ... nothing," she said as she slipped the pea into the pocket of her duffel bag. "Just something that fell into my shoe."

"Hey, nice game Friday night," Barb said as she turned back to Anna.

"No hard feelings—you sure?" asked Anna.

"Are you kidding? Did you see the state rankings in the city paper this morning?" When Anna shook her head, Barb filled her in. "We moved up from ninth to third, and Coleman dropped to number five. I'll take a win like that over starting any day."

"How about Jamie?" asked Anna. "I know she wasn't too thrilled with the lineup change."

"Ah, just give her a little time." Barb forced a note of confidence into her voice. "Jamie'll come around." She pulled on her shoe and started toward the gym door. "We better get out there, or we'll both be benched!"

Jamie was in the middle of her warm-up shooting when she saw Barb and Anna trotting out of the locker room door. Barb headed in Jamie's direction. Jamie picked up her basketball and jogged over to talk to Coach Kelley by the water fountain. Barb slowed to a stop. A few minutes later, a whistle blast summoned them to center court. Coach Miller paced in front of the players as Bernie led them through their warm-up routine.

"Do you know how proud I am of you?" the head coach addressed the group as they bent to their stretches. She answered their grins with a warning. "Just remember now: this means that target on our backs has gotten even bigger. Before we were just the defending league champs. All of a sudden now we're number three in the state."

Whoops and cheers erupted at this. "Now comes the *real* challenge. Keeping our focus, not getting cocky, not getting sloppy, not thinking we have the game won just by stepping onto the court."

The coach stopped her pacing. She waited till all 11 pairs of eyes met hers. "I know you're all thinking about the big showdown with Mason a week from tomorrow. I *know* you are, because I'm guilty, too. They're undefeated in the league, just like we are. It's a big game, but we've got two league games before that one, tomorrow and Friday, and those aren't automatic wins. A loss in either one could really hurt us down the road. I don't give a hoot for the ratings. It's the league record that decides if we get into the playoffs. And even a number one ranking would mean absolutely zippo if we can't win the conference."

The coach paused to let her words sink in. "I know that tomorrow night's game looks like a cinch," she continued. "Twin Lake hasn't won a league game yet this year, but we can't take anybody for granted in this conference. And a championship team brings their best game every night, regardless of the opponent. Let's be that team. Are we ready to make it happen?"

A chorus of cheers assured the coach they were ready to do whatever it took. "Okay!" she answered. "Two laps, and then we get down to business!" «

CHAPTER TWENTY-TWO

FRIDAY NIGHT THE HALFTIME LOCKER room was almost silent as Coach Miller paced angrily in front of the team seated on folding chairs in front of her. "I don't know *what's* come over this team!" she exclaimed. "One week ago tonight we beat the defending state champions, and then four days later we almost lose to the worst team in the league!" She smacked a fist into her palm. "In fact, we probably *should* have lost to Twin Lake, the way we played on Tuesday."

The coach stopped her pacing momentarily. The force of her stare brought the bowed heads up to face the glare. "And then tonight." the coach went on. "Down by six after a first half I wouldn't give two cents for. On our own home court!"

After a pause to let that fact sink in, she continued. "Part of it is the hope we gave to Winnebago by looking so beatable at Twin Lake. Yes, it's true that Winnebago is playing inspired ball tonight. And they're a good team. But I am *not* seeing *my* team, the team I know, out there against them tonight. We look tentative. We're not communicating. We're making careless turnovers, not scrapping for the loose balls."

She lifted her hand to point at a player. "Jamie—what's with you forgetting to call 'shot'—*twice!*"

Jamie hung her head and looked intently at her fingernails.

"And you're not the only one." The head coach looked around the circle of players. "That's why we've given up—" she glanced at the clipboard held out for her by Coach Kelley "*six* offensive rebounds already in *one half!*"

"And Anna," the coach continued, "you've passed up three open shots just in the last five minutes. We need you to be a scorer out there."

Coach Miller sighed, then straightened her shoulders. "Okay. Enough yelling. I know the schedule's been tough on you. This is our first game at home out of the last five we've played. But we go right back on the road for our next two, so we need to learn to play over our fatigue.

"Look at it this way: all this playing away from home right now is good practice for the postseason. And I *am* confident that's still where we're headed, despite whatever it is that's gotten into this team this past week." She gestured to her assistant to take over.

Coach Kelley stepped up, for the moment ignoring her usual station at the board. "All that we've worked so hard for since last March is on the line now," she said. "All great teams reach a point in the season where their commitment is questioned, their desire put to the test. We are at that point now, girls.

"Believe it or not, it's been relatively easy for us so far. We're undefeated in the conference, 10–1 overall, ranked third in the state. Yes, we've worked hard for it." She raised her voice a notch. "But none of it means anything if we let down now."

She turned to the blackboard and raised her chalk. She stood a moment facing the board, then turned back to the circle of solemn faces.

"No," she said, dropping the chalk into her pocket and dusting off her hands. "You all know by now what you need to do out there. We've practiced all the plays, done all the drills, heard the scouting reports. It's the little things that are killing us, not anything I can diagram for you on a blackboard. Let's pull together here and get our attention back on the court where it belongs."

The assistant coach let her glance linger a moment on Jamie, then Anna, then Barb, before she stepped aside to give the floor back to her boss.

"I don't think there's any more that needs to be said." Coach Miller put out her hand and called the team to their feet. "On three," she said. "*Commitment!*" «

CHAPTER TWENTY-THREE

Torrington Loses Shocker to Winnebago
Rally falls short; T-Birds lose game and key player

By Erin Melby
The Thunderbird Press

TORRINGTON—Facing their first serious league challenge as they trailed the Winnebago Falcons at the half, the third-ranked Thunderbirds burst out of their locker room after halftime and quickly erased a six-point deficit.

"We knew what we needed to do," said Torrington head coach Sharon Miller. "And we did it to perfection, too—at least until Millie Meyer went down."

A nine-point T-bird lead early in the fourth quarter seemed to ensure the home team their eighth straight conference victory. The team's poise was shattered, however, when star center Meyer crashed to the floor following a fierce fight for a rebound.

Play stopped for 10 minutes as Meyer, in obvious pain and clutching her left knee, was helped off the floor. Local physician Larry Crispin examined the injured player on the sideline, then called for an ambulance to take her to Barnesville County Hospital for tests. "We won't know the results for a day or so," Dr. Crispin said, "but we're all hoping it's just a bad sprain."

The loss of their interior stopper clipped the wings of the high-flying Thunderbirds. "We were just shocked," said twin sister Mollie. "Millie never gets hurt. She's tough as they come. Bernie did a great job filling in for her, but the rest of us just kind of fell apart."

Despite the letdown and numerous ensuing turnovers, Torrington seemed to regain its composure just in time to save the game. Trailing by only a point with eight seconds to go, sophomore sensation Anna Kiefer's feisty defense pried the ball loose from a stalling Falcon offense. Guard Tina Behrens chased down the loose ball and raced up court for an uncontested layup.

The shot missed the mark, however, and replacement center Luskey saw the ball slip through her hands on the rebound. Time expired as the jubilant Winnebago players recovered the mishandled ball and held on for the win.

The loss puts Torrington a game down on undefeated conference leader Mason going into their showdown on the Bobcats' home court next Tuesday. The T-birds then commence the second half of conference play at league contender Arlington (8–3, 6–2) on Friday.

Jamie eyed the practice court as she walked toward the ball bin while pulling her hair back into a ponytail. Snapping the rubber band into place, she grabbed a basketball and headed over to the side basket where Jeri was practicing her post moves. Jamie nodded over toward the main court, where Bernie and Amy stood talking to the coaches. "I see Amy's been brought up from JV," Jamie said to Jeri. "That's probably not a good sign, eh?"

Jeri shook her head. "Nope. Especially not with the big game with Mason coming up tomorrow. And the news gets worse. Mollie's not here today. I just heard that Millie had surgery on her knee—a torn ligament, I think they said—late this morning. Moll's over at the hospital with her."

"Bummer!" exclaimed Jamie. "Guess you might be needing those post moves if Millie's gone for the season."

"That's kind of what I was thinking," Jeri said grimly as she lofted a hook shot over an imaginary defender. She caught the ball as it dropped cleanly through the net. "With an injury like that, she'll probably be lucky if she can rehab in time to play next year in college. And she and Moll were so excited to both get scholarship offers from Winona State."

A guarded look in Jeri's eyes caused Jamie to turn and look behind her. Barb was approaching, casually dribbling a ball. "You both heard the news?" she asked. When the two juniors nodded, Barb added, "I've got Mom's van today, and I called to ask her if I could drive a bunch of us over to see Millie at the hospital after practice. We should be able to get there in time for a quick visit before they shut down visiting hours over dinnertime. Want to come?"

"Sure," answered Jeri. "You got enough room?"

"Oh, yeah," replied Barb. "We can fit eight in the van, and so far it's just me, Bernie, Emma, Brenda, and Anna."

"Count me in then," said Jeri.

Jamie had already turned back to her practice shooting, but she paused long enough to say, "I think I'll wait and go over tonight. Mom teaches a night class at Shelby on Mondays, so I can hitch a ride over to Barnesville with her." As Jamie resumed her shooting stance she added over her shoulder, "It's probably better for Millie to get company in small doses anyway, being just out of surgery."

Barb looked at her friend with a sigh. "We'll tell the twins to look for you on the second shift, then. Just don't stay out too late. Everybody needs to be at full strength for tomorrow night's game."

"Thanks for the advice." The sarcasm in Jamie's voice was plain to hear. A pained look came over Jeri's face as she tried to come up with a remark to break the uncomfortable silence. A whistle blast knifed through the stalled conversation, and the three players jogged over to join their teammates at center court.

« « « T » » »

Jamie pushed open the heavy hospital room door. The stark white room contained two metal-framed beds separated by a half-drawn curtain.

"Hi, Millie. What's doin'?" chirped Jamie with a forced cheerfulness.

The injured girl grimaced as she pointed to her swollen, bandaged left knee. From a chair beside the bed, Mollie answered for her twin. "The surgery went well. At least they were able to repair the ligament. The surgeon thinks she should be able to play again."

"Might take as long as a year, though," Millie added mournfully. "*Damn!*" The cuss word startled Jamie, coming from the normally straitlaced center.

"Sorry," Millie apologized. "It's just that I—we—had counted so much on getting that championship this year." She looked at Jamie, then quickly added, "Not that the rest of you can't still do that, of course."

Millie gave her twin a glance before turning back to the Jamie. "It's just that the two of us had always dreamed of getting there together, you know? Just like you and Barb."

Jamie nodded, understanding exactly what she meant. "Yeah," she said uncomfortably, "but you'll still be with us on the bench, once you get out of this place. I know it won't be exactly the same, but we need you there with us, you know. You're still a captain— don't think this gets you out of *that* responsibility!"

"Speaking of which ... " Mollie began from her seat beside the bed.

"Huh?" said Jamie, afraid of what was coming.

"We were meaning to talk to you about something," the seated twin continued.

"Yeah, and we probably shouldn't have waited this long," added her sister from her pillow-propped perch on the bed. "We just kept thinking you two would work it out, not let it interfere with the team."

"Oh," said Jamie, her fears confirmed. "You mean me and Barb, I guess."

"Obviously," agreed the sisters in chorus. They looked at each other, then Mollie continued. "I know you felt bad about the way things happened, with that captains' meeting and Barb not telling you ahead of time about her decision to ask the coaches to start Anna in her place." Mollie waved off Jamie's attempt to interrupt. "No, let us finish. You need to hear this."

Millie nodded vigorously in agreement. She flinched as she shifted her leg, trying in vain to find a more comfortable position. Despite the face-whitening pain, she took over the lecture from her sister. "Barb feels terrible, too, you know. She knows she let you down, not trusting you enough to tell you beforehand."

"I think she just felt she had to take the leap before she lost her nerve," interjected Mollie.

"Like when you have to jump off the high-dive board in swimming class, you know?" added Millie. Jamie looked anything but convinced, but she managed to stay quiet.

"You need to talk to her, Jamie," beseeched Mollie. "She's totally broken up about this. The friendship you two have—"

"*Had!*" interrupted Jamie bitterly.

Mollie ignored the outburst. "What you two have is something too special to walk away from."

"Yeah," agreed Millie. "If anybody could understand, it would be us. In fact, we've always said you two were almost like twins, too."

Jamie couldn't hold back a snort of disagreement. "Then why would she do something like that?" she argued. "Like you just said, if anybody could understand, it should be you guys."

Mollie had had enough. "Look, Jamie. Get over it. Barb was just trying to do what she thought was right. And it *was* right—for the team. It was just your loyalty to her that kept you from seeing it like everybody else did."

"And where's that loyalty now, when Barb really needs it?" asked Millie, unable to keep a note of harshness from her voice. "Not only that, but the way you're behaving is affecting the whole team. You're distracted, Barb is devastated, Anna feels so guilty it's affecting her play."

"And everybody on the team feels like they've got to tiptoe around the two of you," Mollie added. "Either you figure out a way to swallow your pride and patch this up, *soon,* or it's going to be too late to save either the season *or* your friendship."

Jamie turned her face toward the door, trying to hide the quivering of her bottom lip and the tears welling in her eyes. Mollie got up from her chair and came over to wrap Jamie in a big hug.

« « « 𝕋 » » »

Jamie waited on the broad stone step in front of the hospital for her mom to pick her up. A gust of wind blew a shower of snow off the flat roof above her. Jamie watched morosely as the snowflakes swirled through the shaft of light streaming from the big spotlight over the doors.

Tugging off a mitten, she reached inside the neck of her parka and brought out a thin gold chain. A beam of headlights washed across the steps, creating a momentary flash of red from the eyes of the golden thunderbird in Jamie's hand. The twins were right. Saving her stubborn pride was not worth losing her best friend, and the fallout was clearly poisoning the season for the whole team.

By the time her mother pulled the car up to the curb, Jamie was on her feet and reaching for the handle of the passenger door.

"Want to make a quick stop at the Dairy Queen on the way home?" offered Mrs. Johnson.

"No thanks, Mom—not tonight," replied Jamie. "I need to get home to make a phone call." ◀

CHAPTER TWENTY-FOUR

"IT'S FOR YOU!" hollered Rosie.

Barb laid her pencil down on the math book open in front of her. "Who is it?" she mouthed to her sister, glancing at her wristwatch as she pushed her chair back from the kitchen table.

Rosie put a hand over the mouthpiece of the phone. "Sounds like Jamie," she whispered.

With a look of surprise, Barb took the phone from her little sister and waved her out of the room. "Hello?" she said tentatively into the phone.

"Hi. It's me. You busy?"

"Uh, just finishing a set of homework problems for tomorrow," replied Barb.

"Can I come over for a few minutes?"

"Now? I mean ... well ... sure." After a moment of awkward silence, she forced a casual tone. "What's up? I mean, you haven't been over here for a while."

"You've got something of mine that I need to get back."

"Oh." The hopeful look on Barb's face disappeared. "And what might that be?"

"Well ..." came the reply. "It's small and round and green and comes in pairs." A pause, then Jamie's voice resumed. "I think maybe I lost it in your shoe at practice last week." «

CHAPTER TWENTY-FIVE

FOUR THUNDERBIRDS STARTERS already stood at Mason's center court in their blue away uniforms. They listened as the announcer completed their lineup: *"And at center,"* the voice rang out, *"Number 50, Bernadette Luskey!"*

Mollie reached up to slap Bernie's big paws. Anna, Tina, and Jamie followed suit, then pulled the nervous first-time starter into a quick huddle. The big crowd of Torrington fans in the visitors' section roared as Mollie strained to be heard over their cheers. "This is it, gang," shouted Mollie. "Redemption time. Let's go get 'em!"

The rising tension made the home team introductions seem to last forever as the Thunderbird starters stood facing the bleachers. Finally the last Mason starter took the floor to thunderous applause. The Torrington quintet clapped along politely, then broke for the sideline to join their waiting teammates.

The players gathered around the two coaches for their usual last-minute instructions. "I don't need to tell you this is a big one," began the head coach. "A win here and we're back in control of our own destiny. A win ties us with Mason for the league lead; a loss, and we have to hope for somebody else in the conference to save us by knocking them off. And we don't want that, do we?"

"*No!!!*" came the unanimous response.

"All right, then," said the coach, satisfied that her troops were ready for the challenge. "Let's just get out there and do what we know we can do."

The crowd quieted as the teams faced the flag for the national anthem. As the last of the recorded strains died away, a renewed roar erupted from the packed house. A whistle blast called the teams onto the court.

Barb hurriedly gathered the team for its pre-game cheer. "Let's win this one for Millie," she urged. "She'll be listening on the radio. Let's make sure she hears some good news to cheer up that gloomy hospital room!" Barb stuck out her hand. Jamie's hand smacked down on top of it, then Mollie's. As the rest of the palms piled on, Barb ordered, "On three, *dominate!*"

Bernie's nervous energy produced a center jump that startled even her. Anna chased down the spiked ball, then fed it ahead to Tina. A faked jumper turned into a lob pass to an unguarded Mollie, and Torrington had the first lead.

Mason responded with a furious charge up the court as the Thunderbirds scrambled to find their matchups. Two crisp passes, then a third. A shot arced toward the rim. Five blue uniforms whirled to box out five white ones as a cry of "Shot!" echoed over the court.

A long rebound caromed into Anna's waiting hands. An outlet pass to

Jamie triggered a textbook fastbreak. Jamie raced the ball up the middle of the court, keeping an eye on Tina and Mollie filling the lanes at either side. Jamie pulled up at the free throw line, keeping her dribble alive as she scanned for an open teammate. Mollie called for the ball with a hand held high as she cut through the key. Jamie faked a pass in her direction, then flicked a sideways no-look pass to Anna following in her wake. The sophomore scorer wasted no time making it a four-point lead for the visiting team.

Jamie slapped Anna's hand as they raced back on defense. "Nice shot, Slick!" Jamie hollered. Anna shot her a surprised look, then grinned and gave a thumbs-up in reply.

Five minutes into the first quarter, the beleaguered Bobcats called a timeout. As the white and red uniforms clustered around the gesticulating Mason coaches, the visiting team jumped and screamed from the opposite bench.

"That ought to cheer your sister up," a relieved Bernie commented to Mollie as they ran for the sideline. "12–4 already!"

Mollie pumped her fist in the air in jubilation. "Good start, Bern!" she crowed. "Now we've just got to keep it up for the rest of the game!"

The timeout pulled the home team out of their daze. The Mason fans roared their approval as the Bobcats slowly gained ground on the Thunderbirds. A nothing-but-net three-pointer pulled the home team even just before the first quarter ended.

Coach Miller wasted no time during the brief break between periods. "We're still on track here. No need to panic," she reassured her anxious team. "They're hitting everything they throw up there right now, but we're playing good defense, and they can't keep up that percentage all night," she said, hoping to herself that she was right.

Coach Kelley stepped in to correct a few flaws in the defense as the head coach gauged the condition of her current lineup. "Jeri, report in for Bernie," she said when her assistant had finished. "And Anna, you're back in for Barb."

The reinforcements raced to the scorer's table as Mollie, Tina, and Jamie took the floor. "I think we're wearing them down a little already," remarked Tina to Jamie as they got set to start the second quarter.

"For sure," agreed the point guard. "Let's keep pushing the pace. No way they can keep up with us for a whole game!"

By halftime the Thunderbirds had clawed their way back to a five-point advantage. As the blue team emerged from their locker room for second-half warm-ups, Erin Melby cornered the pair of coaches. "Any scoop for your favorite sideline reporter?" she asked hopefully.

Coach Miller gave the halftime stat sheet a final glance, then handed her clipboard to her assistant and waved her on toward the bench. "Now Erin," she chided the pencil-poised girl walking backwards in front of her. "You of all people should know better than to try to talk to us during the game!"

"I know, Coach, but just this once ... " she wheedled. "The *Torrington Times* is giving me a big column in the city paper tomorrow—front page of the sports section! My second one this season!"

The coach stopped, then reached out to gently close Erin's notebook. "After the game, Erin," she said firmly. "But I promise you we'll do our best to make sure you have a good story to write then." She gave the girl a friendly clap on the elbow, then hurried to the bench. ≪

CHAPTER TWENTY-SIX

WEDNESDAY MORNING, Jamie headed over to rehash the game with Barb before their recently resumed morning trek to school. Jamie lounged in the faded green chair re-reading Erin's front-page article in the Torrington newspaper while Barb peered over her shoulder from her perch on the chair's arm. Absorbed in their reading, neither girl heard the door creak open at the bottom of the stairs.

"Mom says come down for breakfast!" called Rosie. "*Right now.*"

"Okay, okay, Little Bit," said Barb. "Hold your horses. We'll be there in just a minute."

Jamie stifled a yawn as she stretched her arms. "Well, Barb," she said, "looks like Erin got a good story, anyway. I just wish it had a better ending."

"Me, too," said Barb. "Me, too." She picked up the paper, glancing again at the headline.

Fouls cost Thunderbirds; Bobcats build 2-game lead in conference race

By Erin Melby
For the Torrington Times

MASON—The season that began with such high hopes for the Torrington Thunderbirds may have seen its promise shattered last night on the home floor of the Mason Bobcats.

Early in the game, Torrington seemed to have erased the damage caused last week by the loss of senior center Millie Meyer to a season-ending knee injury. The Thunderbirds came out firing on all cylinders, quickly building a 12–4 lead behind solid if unspectacular post play from replacement center Bernie Luskey.

A timeout by Mason at the five-minute mark helped the Bobcats shut down the early hot shooting of T-bird star Anna Kiefer, and the home team scratched their way back to an 18–18 tie by the end of the first quarter.

Torrington coach Sharon Miller tried to counter the Bobcats' focus on Kiefer by replacing her with former starting forward Barb McMahon, but the senior co-captain wasn't able to find her range. "McMahon helped us regain our composure on defense," noted the coach, "but her shot just wasn't falling."

Sophomore shooting guard Tina Behrens rallied the Thunderbirds in the second quarter of play, scoring on several drives while dishing out four assists. She also teamed with Kiefer for a combined five steals in the period, the fruit of a furious full-court press. The pressure defense led to several easy baskets off turnovers, giving Torrington a five-point advantage by halftime.

Unfortunately for the visitors, the press also produced a rash of fouls, leaving point guard Jamie Johnson and Luskey each with three by the half.

"The press was rattling them, so I hated to abandon it," commented Coach Miller after the game. In a surprise move, Miller opened the second half with backup guard Kelly Carter at the point and freshman JV call-up Amy Knudson at center. "I didn't want to back off on the press," explained the coach, "so I thought we'd try throwing in some fresh troops."

The tactic worked for a time, as the visiting team built their lead to nine. Fouls continued to plague the Thunderbirds, however, forcing the coach to call off the press by the end of the third quarter.

"We had six team fouls already," noted the coach. "I knew we'd be facing a bonus situation at the free throw line most of the fourth quarter as it was, and I knew we'd need Jamie back in to run the offense down the stretch."

Mason's stellar 83% free throw shooting for the game helped narrow the gap in the final period. With Mason trailing by just three and under a minute remaining, Johnson's fifth foul put Bobcat ace Terri Dutton on the line.

Dutton canned the shot, completing a three-point play and pulling the home team into a tie for the first time since the opening quarter.

With Johnson and Luskey both lost to fouls, Torrington couldn't break the tie and the game went into overtime. Kiefer recovered her shooting touch, however, and staked the Thunderbirds to a four-point lead midway through the extra period.

A controversial offensive charging call then put the sophomore scorer on the bench for good, the first time all season that Kiefer has fouled out of a game.

A patchwork lineup of Carter and Behrens at the guards, McMahon and Mollie Meyer at forward, and Jeri Swanson in the post kept the Thunderbirds in the game as the overtime period wound down. The situation looked grim, however, when the Bobcats took possession of the basketball with six seconds to go and a one-point lead.

The Thunderbirds weren't about to concede to their rivals, despite the desperate situation. McMahon stripped Dutton of the ball, leading the Mason star to commit an ill-advised foul.

On the line to shoot two, McMahon swished the first shot, only to have the basket cancelled as the official called teammate Meyer for entering the lane early. McMahon's second shot missed the mark, and Mason recovered the ball as time expired.

"I wouldn't count us out of the race quite yet,"

admonished Coach Miller. "We may be down two games to Mason, but the second half of the season's just starting. A lot can happen with nine games to go. There's more than just two good teams in the league this year. We just need a little help from a couple of them now."

The anticipated final showdown between Torrington and Mason on the last night of league play a month from now may prove to be a bust, however, unless another conference team can mount a threat to the front-running Bobcats. That challenge could come as soon as this Friday, when Mason faces league upstart Winnebago. The Falcons pulled off the surprise of the season in the Valley Conference by beating Torrington last week.

Up next for the 9–3, 7–2 Thunderbirds is a rematch with 8–4, 6–3 Arlington. Although the Thunderbirds handled the Spartans easily in their first meeting back in December, Arlington has also emerged as a conference contender, and this game will be played on the Spartans' home court.

The stairway door opened again. "Barbara Ann, Jamie Lynn!" called Mrs. McMahon. "I've got bacon and eggs on the table down here, and you've got exactly 15 minutes before you have to leave for school!"

"Coming, Mom," answered Barb as she stood up and swatted the newspaper out of Jamie's hands.

Jamie retrieved the paper and crumpled it into a ball before launching it into the wastebasket. "What a bunch of rotten breaks," she exclaimed as she pushed herself to her feet. "First, Anna fouls out, which she never *ever* does, on a bad charging call, no less. And then that weird thing with Mollie losing her balance on the lane and spoiling your free throw at the end of the game."

"It sure was a bad-luck ending, right when I thought we finally had the momentum going our way. But if only I'd made that second shot. That would have at least gotten us a second overtime."

"And almost nobody left to play it with!" reminded Jamie. "Don't beat yourself up over that. If it wasn't for your steal in the first place, we'd never have even had that last chance to pull off the win."

"I suppose you're right."

"Of course I'm right. Now we just need for that ol' Thunderbird to shoot some of his thunderbolts in Mason's direction for a change. I think we've more than had our share."

Barb face turned serious as she nodded thoughtfully. "Yeah, I just hope it's not too late. I sure never thought we'd be struggling so hard just to get back into the *conference* race, especially this early in the season."

"*Girls!*" a voice boomed. "Now! I mean it!"

"We're there, Mrs. McMahon!" Jamie called out as they pounded down the stairs. To the back of Barb's head she added, "There's still time to come back. Next up, Arlington. One game at a time."

"And who sounds like a captain now?" teased her friend as she flicked off the light switch at the bottom of the stairway. «

CHAPTER *TWENTY-SEVEN*

AS ASSISTANT COACH KELLY was winding up her pre-game review of the defensive plan in the visitors' locker room before the Arlington game, the door leading to the court had opened a crack. Now a crutch tip pushed it wide open. A surprised cheer rose from the crew inside the room.

Coach Miller gave the intruder a knowing smile as she waited for the uproar to die down. "Welcome back, Millie!" she said when she could finally make herself heard. "You're just in time to give us a few words of wisdom before we head out for warm-ups."

The hobbled center beamed at her teammates. "I got back as soon as I could," she told them. "After the way the last two games went, I figured you needed a super-size good-luck mascot with you on the bench." Her demeanor turned serious as she waved her right crutch toward the door.

"I want you all to run onto that court tonight with *fire* in your eyes. Never let them even *think* they can stay in this game with you."

The players rose to their feet, clapping and whistling. The head coach nodded to Millie, who waved her crutch again to quiet the ovation. "Everybody over here," she commanded, dropping her crutch back down to the floor and holding out her hand. As her teammates crowded in to plop their hands over hers, the injured co-captain called out the cheer: "On three, *smoke 'em!*"

The words rang out; the huddle broke. Coach Kelley held open the door as the fired-up squad raced for the court. After the last player cleared the doorway, Coach Miller followed slowly as Millie limped beside her. "Good to have you back, Millie," the head coach said as she ushered the injured co-captain out the door.

"Thanks, Coach. It's good to be here. And thanks for letting me butt in on your pre-game talk."

"I'm not above a little melodrama when the situation calls for it," replied the coach with a wry smile. "Let's just hope it works!"

The families of the Torrington players had staked out their usual away-game territory in the top three rows of the visitors' section. Next to the trio of Johnsons stood the Kiefer family, all decked out in Torrington blue. Behind them the McMahon clan stood four strong. Mr. Johnson reached back to shake Barb's older sister's hand. "I see you made it home for the weekend, Colleen!" he shouted over the uproar.

"I wanted to come last Tuesday," replied the college student. "But I had a class I just couldn't afford to miss."

"That's OK," said Jason Johnson, fiddling with a wire dangling from his ear. "I'm wagering that this game will be considerably more pleasant to watch than that debacle was, anyway."

"Let's hope so!" said Mrs. McMahon, smiling at her godson's vocabulary as she squeezed her oldest daughter's arm.

The crowd hushed as the announcer began to call out the starting lineups. Jason took advantage of the silence to tune in an FM station on his homemade Heathkit radio receiver. "Got it!" he exclaimed, pressing the headphones firmly over his ears.

"Game boring you already, son?" asked Mr. Johnson.

"No," replied the boy, pushing his glasses back up his nose. "I just figured we might want to keep abreast of how Mason's doing against the Falcons. The game just started—no score yet," he reported.

"Well, you keep us posted," said Mr. McMahon, reaching forward to pat the young techno-wizard on the shoulder. "If you can hear anything over this noise, that is!"

The lineups complete, the anthem over, the game finally got under way. The Thunderbirds carried their pre-game fireworks with them onto the court. They sprinted to an early lead, then gradually built the margin to 15 points as halftime approached.

Jason stationed himself down at the edge of the stands as the clock ticked down, hoping to catch his sister's eye as the team headed to the locker room for the break. Millie spotted Jason's futile waving just as the last Thunderbird player raced past him without stopping. She called out to the frustrated boy just as he turned resignedly back toward the bleachers. "What's up, Jason?"

As Jason turned to locate the voice, Millie clumped the rest of the way over to him. "Just thought you guys might like some reconnaissance on the Mason–Winnebago game," Jason replied, tapping his headphones.

"You got some good news for us then?" asked Millie, leaning forward on her crutches.

Jason looked up at the form towering over him, then shook his head. "Afraid not," he admitted. "They're just getting ready to start the second half, and Mason's up by eight."

"Hmm ..." said Millie. "That's no good. But Winnebago's tough. They came back on us when they were down by nine last week, and with only a quarter to go, you remember."

"Yes," came the skeptical reply. "But *that* might have had something to do with their comeback." Jason pointed at the bulky blue and white immobilizer velcroed around Millie's left leg.

Millie reached down to tousle the boy's hair. "Thanks for the vote of confidence," she said with a grin. "I think I'll just sit on that news for now, though. Better if we let the team just keep their attention on what they can control here on this floor."

"You're probably right," Jason conceded. "But I'll keep monitoring the radio, just in case."

"You do that," replied Millie as she headed to the locker room. "You can fill us in after the game," she called back over her shoulder.

By the end of the third quarter, a 20-point margin had subdued the fans in Arlington green and white. A relaxed atmosphere reigned in the visitors' stands as a lineup of lesser-known faces took the floor to start the final period. "Congratulations, Maria!" said Mrs. McMahon to Mrs. Kiefer. "Looks like the starters are done for the night, but my tally shows 21 points for Anna." She waved her pen-marked program.

"Thank you, Maggie," said Anna's mother with a pleased blush. "And your daughter's had a good night, too! And yours, Katie," she added, turning to Mrs. Johnson.

"It's been a good night for everybody," agreed Jamie's mom. "It's nice to see the whole team get some playing time." She gestured to the subs running a fastbreak down on the court below. "And what a relief to see the girls play like this after all the trials of the last couple weeks!"

"Now if only they can just keep it up for eight more games." said Barb's dad.

"And if only somebody'd help us by knocking off Mason." added Mr. Johnson.

"Speaking of which, where's our little radio reporter?" asked Colleen McMahon. "He was just here a minute ago."

A small hand plucked at Millie's sleeve from behind her seat at the end of the bench. She twisted awkwardly to look over her shoulder. "Jason!" she stage-whispered. "What are you doing here?"

The boy gestured excitedly to the radio. "Winnebago is catching up!" he exclaimed. "Down three with a minute and a half to go!"

Millie hushed him with a warning finger to her lips, then waved him to a kneeling position on the strip of open floor behind her. "Stay there!" she ordered. "And give me one of those headphones!" she added.

The large head and the small one huddled together, temporarily oblivious to the action on the floor in front of them. If anyone noticed the sudden exchange of hand slaps between the two a few moments later, they might have chalked it up to the events out on the court. The second-stringers had extended the Thunderbird lead to 25.

As time expired on the big game clock, Millie hobbled over toward the scorer's table. A moment later the announcer's voice boomed over the loudspeakers. "*This just in from Winnebago. The Falcons have defeated the Mason Bobcats!"*

The blue side of the orderly lines of handshaking players rushed through the post-game ritual, then exploded to the sideline to surround Millie Meyer in a knee-endangering group hug. "Whoa!" laughed Millie as she backed up against the scorer's table and spread her crutches in a protective stance. "Watch that bum leg!"

Coach Miller finally managed to make herself heard over the celebration. "Listen up for a minute here!" she began when the cheering subsided. "I don't want to pull you back into the locker room right now because there's some proud families and fans waiting to celebrate with you out there." She gestured to the blue-and-gold crowd gathering under the far basket. "I just want to say a couple quick things. Then you can head over to see them."

"First, you played an *excellent* game tonight." A renewed burst of cheers greeted her comment. "Second, we got a little help from our friends the Falcons tonight." More cheers, a few whistles.

"Now we need to capitalize on that boost." The coach looked around the happy throng of faces. "Remember we have an off-night next Tuesday— no game until Friday, a week from today. You've all been working so hard, I think we deserve a little break. We'll practice as usual on Monday, but I'm giving you Tuesday off."

Reacting to the looks of disbelief, she continued, "Now, if you decide to go over to Barnesville that night to scout our opponents for Friday's game, that's up to you ..." The puzzled looks dissolved in happy laughter. ❮

CHAPTER *TWENTY-EIGHT*

THE BLUE-AND-GOLD LETTER-JACKETED GANG stood just inside the doorway of the Barnesville gym. "The coaches are up there," noted Bernie, pointing to the last row on the opposite side. "But I don't see any empty seats up by them."

Jeri looked in the direction Bernie had indicated. "They probably deserve a break from us for one night, anyway."

"Hey," said Emma, interrupting the chuckles. "Isn't that Karin the lab lady up there?" The players' heads turned toward the top of the bleachers where Emma was pointing.

"Looks like her," agreed Jeri.

Their energetic waving caught the graduate student's attention. She waved back and gestured to the empty row behind her. Mollie signaled back, then told the rest of the team, "You guys go on up there to sit. Millie and I'll stay down here behind their bench and see if we can pick up any secrets."

As the remaining girls made their way up through the crowd in the bleachers, Kelly tugged at Jamie's jacket. "That wouldn't be that A.J. guy sitting next to Karin, would it? The Shelby College guy from the pickup game?"

"Hey, I think it *is* him!" exclaimed Jamie, squinting up into the stands. "Jeri!" Jamie nudged the player in front of her. "That's the guy whose shirt you scored last summer. Better hide your face!"

The girls stopped in their tracks to wait out the playing of the anthem. By the time the ball was tossed, they had finally reached the empty seats.

"Hey, it's my team!" exclaimed Karin, shaking hands with Barb, Jamie, Emma, Kelly, Amy, and Jeri as they shuffled down the row behind her. Jamie made the introductions to Anna, Bernie, Brenda, and Tina. "Karin works in Mom's lab at Shelby," Jamie explained to the four who had missed the summer adventure on the college campus.

"And she helped your teammates here embarrass the local talent," added A.J., winking at the six girls who had been there.

"Aha!" said Brenda. "Those shirts ..."

"Oh, no!" A.J. cringed. "The legend lives ..."

Karin jumped in to introduce A.J. to the rest of the players. "A.J. here is thinking about trying to break into coaching girls' basketball next season," she added. "So I dragged him along to give him some pointers."

"If you can't beat 'em, join 'em," said the bearded man with a sheepish grin.

Barb interrupted the resounding laughter, pointing to the action on the court. "We better pay attention here," the captain warned.

At halftime, Jamie and Barb took orders from their teammates to make a refreshment run. They stopped behind the Barnesville bench to check in with the twins. "Any good scoop yet?" Barb asked her co-captains.

"Nah, not really," answered Millie as she tried to keep her brace-bound leg out of the line of traffic passing in front of her. "Doesn't seem like they've added much new stuff, except maybe that one out-of-bounds play under their own basket."

"You two want a Coke or anything?" asked Barb.

"Sure," said Mollie, digging in her jeans pocket. She dropped a pair of crumpled dollar bills into Barb's hand. "Two of anything that's not diet."

"Gotcha," said Barb. "We'll be back in a flash."

The two girls shouldered their way through the crowd to the snack stand. As they waited in line, Jamie did a double take. "Hey!" she said in a low voice, trying to be casual as she inclined her head toward an approaching figure. "Isn't that...?"

Barb scrutinized the tall, gangly fellow Jamie was indicating. "I do believe it's Mr. Stringbean!" she whispered back as he neared them. "And look who's with him."

"Hullo, ladies," said Buff Boy, eyeing their team jackets. "Out hunting for more shirts to scam?"

Barb saw the telltale flash in Jamie's eyes. Just as Jamie opened her mouth for a pointed reply, Barb stepped firmly on her foot. "Just out scouting the opposition for Friday," Barb answered for both of them. "We didn't have a game scheduled for tonight. You guys follow the Barnesville team?"

Buff Boy puffed up his chest. "You bet!" he answered. "My girlfriend's on the team."

"Mine, too," added Stringbean.

"So I guess we'll be seeing you at our gym next game," said Jamie, rubbing her foot.

"Yup," said Stringbean cheerfully. "Rooting against you all the way!"

"Come on, Mike," said Buff Boy. "It's almost time for the second half."

"Good luck to your team tonight," called Barb diplomatically as the pair turned to leave.

"And thanks for the shirts!" added Jamie devilishly as the boys faded into the crowd.

Laden with paper cups in cardboard holders, the two girls made their way back to the stands. They reached the Meyer sisters just as the second half tipped off. As the twins relieved them of two soft drinks, Jamie and Jules hunkered down in the aisle in front of them to await the next stoppage in play.

"Wonder which ones are their girlfriends?" said Jamie.

Barb shrugged. "Don't know. I imagine they'll hear about our scouting expedition, though. I s'pose they've already heard plenty about last summer's pickup game. A little extra incentive for them against us on Friday. Besides avenging that first loss to us, I mean."

Jamie considered this, sipping her pop as she followed the action on the court. "Well, *we* certainly can't afford another loss," she replied. "No matter what their incentive!"

A whistle sounded. Jamie and Barb used the break in the action to scamper back up to their seats at the top of the stands. They passed out the rest of the drinks, along with their news about A.J.'s erstwhile teammates.

"Hey, I just played with them one day, for that one round of games," protested A.J. "I'm in your corner now. Always go with the winner, I say!"

"Some would call that fair weather friendship," commented Karin.

"Huh?" said A.J.

"Never mind," replied Karin. "Just watch the game." «

CHAPTER TWENTY-NINE

Thunderbirds Crush Carson City Comets
Torrington stretches streak to 6; Mason maintains lead

By Erin Melby
The Thunderbird Press

TORRINGTON—The big dose of adversity they weathered last month seems to have prepared Torrington's roundballers for any obstacle down the stretch. Ever since a season-ending injury to starting center Millie Meyer triggered back-to-back losses last month, the Thunderbirds have looked invincible while stringing together six straight conference wins.

Last night's 79–48 victory over Carson City was never in doubt despite the loss of sophomore guard Tina Behrens to an ankle sprain in the first half of play.

"We didn't miss a beat," commented Coach Sharon Miller. "Kiefer moved over to shooting guard, and McMahon stepped back in at the small forward spot. Of course, we're all glad that Behrens won't be out of commission long—Dr.

Crispin says she should be able to practice in a day or two—but I think we've learned the lesson that the success of this team doesn't depend on any one person."

Continuing a pattern set in recent games with Barnesville and Eagleton, Torrington turned to its second string to preserve a large second-half lead.

"Our subs really stepped up for us," said Miller. "The full-court pressure we play really wears down our opponents, but it can also drain our own starters—especially near the end of a long season like this. This way we've been able to get them some rest while getting great game experience for our bench."

The supporting cast came through big on the stat sheet. High scorer for the game was Jeri

Swanson, with 16 points in relief of Mollie Meyer at power forward. Junior backcourt backups Brenda Thorson and Emma Larson combined for four steals and five assists against no turnovers. Freshman center Amy Knudson made efficient use of her 16 minutes of playing time to score 10 points while pulling down eight boards.

Torrington rounds out the conference season with a home game against Twin Lake and a road contest at Winnebago next week before taking on league rival Mason on the final night of the regular season. Mason continues to hold a one-game lead over Torrington, with games at Arlington and Barnesville leading up to the final showdown at Torrington.

The Monday lunchtime crowd was drifting out of the school cafeteria as a crowd of Torrington players huddled over three copies of the school newspaper at their usual table.

"Erin didn't mention the new state rankings," noted Jeri when she finished scanning their former teammate's article. "The poll in yesterday's city paper had us moved back up to tenth."

"Yeah," said Barb, "but a Top 10 ranking's pretty worthless if we don't even make it into the playoffs."

Mollie shook her finger at Barb. "We can't be worrying about the play-offs right now, or even beating Mason next week. If we lose tomorrow's game, or Friday's, none of that will matter anyway."

"Yeah," agreed Jeri. "We all remember the result of taking Twin Lake lightly last time around. And since then, they've actually won a couple games."

"And they'll sure be gunning for us tomorrow night," added Tina.

"How's your ankle, Teenie?" asked Kelly, pointing to the guard's ace wrapped appendage propped up on a chair.

"Oh, it'll be fine," the sophomore answered. She prodded the bandage with her finger, wincing only slightly. "I can put weight on it today. Doc Crispin says that means I can practice." She planted the foot on the floor and stood up gingerly. "Don't think I'll be doing any hard running yet today, though."

"Don't worry, Teen. Anna and Bren and I got you covered," replied Kelly.

A quiet voice piped up from the end of the table. "But if it takes three of us to make up for you being out, you better get back by Friday!"

"Anna's right," concurred Brenda. "Winnebago's still on a roll, ever since they beat us."

"And don't forget, they beat Mason, too!" warned Bernie.

"Yeah, wouldn't that be the kicker—Winnebago knocks us off again, and then we finally beat Mason in the last game, and Winnebago goes to the playoffs!"

"And don't think Winnebago isn't thinking about that!" warned Millie. "We've got two tough games this week before we can even *start* thinking about Mason."

The bell rang. "See you at practice, everybody!" hollered Mollie as they scattered. "Trounce those Titans!" «

CHAPTER THIRTY

THE ATMOSPHERE IN THE visitors' locker room crackled with intensity. Assistant Coach Kelley jabbed a finger at the score circled on the blackboard as she finished up her halftime comments. "A two-point lead—Winnebago's hanging tough with us. No surprise there. We knew we'd be in for a battle tonight, and we're getting it. But you're running the game plan just like we laid it out. Keep with it, and we'll come through. We're wearing them down little by little, and we know our bench is stronger and deeper than theirs."

Coach Miller stepped back in front of the team as her assistant sat down. "Although my nerves might disagree," she said, kneading the back of her neck, "a close game tonight is probably a good thing for us at this point. You've been playing so well that nobody's been able to give us much of a challenge for the past couple weeks. And you're playing great again tonight.

We've just run into a team on a mission. The same mission as ours."

The coach dropped her hand from her neck and looked around the room. Her voice grew quieter yet still penetrated every corner of the room. "I was proud of how you kept your focus against Twin Lake on Tuesday, and I'm proud of the job you're doing tonight. This is what we've worked for, trained for, all year long. A game like this, with everything on the line. Now let's get out there and finish it!"

As the team huddled around the head coach for the cheer, her assistant walked over to the corner of the room where Tina sat alone on a taping table. The skin on the guard's bare left ankle was damp from its halftime soak in an ice bucket. The coach tossed her a towel and picked up a roll of white tape. "How's the ankle feeling, Tina? You going to be able to go again this half?"

"I think so, Coach. It felt fine while I was playing on it; it just stiffened up some when I was sitting."

Tina watched as Coach Kelley expertly ripped lengths of tape and began strapping the contours of her foot. Coach Miller shut the door behind the last of the departing players, then joined the pair in the corner. "What's the word on the foot?" she asked, jiggling the coins in her pocket.

"I'm ready to go as much as you need me this half," declared Tina as the assistant coach finished off the tape job.

"OK," said Coach Miller, with an undisguised sigh of relief. "Get that shoe on and go jog a couple laps around the court to loosen it up before you join the shooting drills."

The school bus rocked with cheers as the last wet-haired players filed through the big folding door at the front. "We did it!" shouted Tina, limping down the aisle. "Eight in a row! Mason, watch out!"

Jamie peered over the bus driver's shoulder as he fiddled with a knob on the bus radio. "No, that's not it. Try over to the right just a little more."

The tinny speaker crackled with static. A voice broke through the noise. "*... in heaven there is no beer, that's why we drink it here.*" Boos and hisses filled the air.

"That's the polka station from New Ulm," hollered Jeri. "The Barnesville station should be the next one up the dial."

The bus driver twisted the knob another half turn. More static. Then a voice. And the unmistakable background sound of cheering in an echoing gymnasium.

"That's it!' said Jamie urgently. "Turn it up! Please!"

"*... and it's Barnesville's ball, trailing by just three points, with just over a minute to go in this second overtime period. And what a game it's been, folks!*"

All of the Torrington players crowded up to the front of the bus. Hands reached for hands as the din of voices instantly subsided.

"*And it's Harrington to Jones in the right corner for Barnesville. Jones looks ... looks ... nothing open. She swings the ball back up to Harrington at the top of the key. Harrington eyes the basket; they're giving her a little room. Will she take the three? Yes! And it's good! Tie ball game!*"

The bus erupted in cheers. "Go Mustangs!" hollered Millie, brandishing a crutch dangerously overhead.

"Shhhh!" hissed her sister. "I can't hear."

"This score just in from Winnebago: Torrington Thunderbirds 75, Winnebago Falcons 67. That means a win by Barnesville here tonight would drop Mason into a tie with Torrington going into their final league game next Tuesday."

More cheers, then a quick hush as the play-by-play resumed.

"Mason's ball. Barnesville back in a two-three zone. All tied at 83. Perry at the point for the Bobcats, taking her time. She's across half court. Thirty-four seconds to go in the game ... or should I say in this second overtime? The way this thing's gone tonight, we may not get a winner till midnight! Mason goes into their half-court set. Perry to Nelson, back to Perry. Twenty-six seconds and counting. The Bobcats are showing great patience, trying to draw the Mustangs out of their zone."

"Come on, Barnesville. Hold 'em!" hollered Emma, squeezing Jamie's shoulder.

"No fouls!" breathed Barb, crouching next to Jamie at the front of the crowded bus. "No fouls!"

The players pushed closer, all eyes on the glowing orange face of the radio, as if watching the dial could somehow help them see the game.

"Barnesville is still hanging back in their zone, daring the Bobcats to put up a long one. Nothing doing. Eighteen seconds ... 17 ... 16 ... Mason's going to have to do something, and soon, if they want to keep this from going into a third extra period. Okay, here it comes. A pass down to Smith in the right corner, she lobs it in to Stinson at the low post. Stinson turns to the baseline. Nothing open there, six seconds to go. She pivots back to the middle. Puts up a left-handed shot. Deflected by Harrington! Harrington blocks the shot! No whistle. Ball still in play, being chased down by Number 23 for Barnesville. She gets a hand on it, pivots, flings it

up toward the Mustang end of the court."

A burst of cheers erupted on the bus, quickly hushed.

" ... and there's Jones, flying ahead on the break for Barnesville. Two on one, Nelson back to defend for Mason. Jones takes the shot ..."

The sound of the buzzer knifed through the radio static.

"This is the game if it goes. It's up. It's on the rim, it's ... GOOD! Barnesville wins the game!" «

CHAPTER *THIRTY-ONE*

THE TORRINGTON GYM WAS PACKED WITH bodies and bursting with noise. Bands from both schools blared fight songs from opposite ends of the bleachers. One side of the stands was a solid sea of Thunderbird blue and gold, the other side awash in Bobcat red and white.

Jamie stood behind Barb at the end of the layup line, jiggling her hands and running in place. "Nervous?" asked Barb.

"Nah," said Jamie, fidgeting. "Well, maybe a little," she admitted. "I just wish we'd get this game started!"

"Me, too," replied Barb. "And I want to make sure this isn't my last game in a Torrington uniform."

The scoreboard clock showed 8:03 left on the pregame countdown. Millie stood under the basket, still in street clothes but off her crutches now, watching the clock. When the big red numbers hit 4:00, she whistled sharply through her fingers. "Free throws!" the command rang out.

Barb stepped to the line as five players settled in on each side of the lane. "Start us off right!" called Millie as she tossed the ball to her co-captain. Barb licked her lips as she eyed the rim. The ball left her fingertips in a soft arc. One for one. Hand slaps all around. Next shooter.

Two minutes later the ritual was complete and the team was jogging over to the coaches waiting on the sideline. "Got 'em all, Coach!" exclaimed Millie as she brought up the rear. "First time all season!"

"Perfect timing," said Coach Miller. "Now let's take that good omen and put it to work!"

Up in the top section of the stands roped off as a press box, Erin Melby sat with her notebook on her knee. *"Torrington wins toss,"* she scribbled as the game got under way. *"Three passes; shot by Kiefer. Miss. Putback, Knudson. 2–0 T-birds."*

A two-teacher stats crew sitting next to Erin captured everything in neat columns on their clipboards. "Who was that foul on?" one of them asked Erin midway through the first quarter.

"Red 42," she replied. "Johnson shooting. Basket was good." Erin turned her attention back to the court. *"Free throw good,"* she wrote. *"Torr. up by 6, 3:23 to go. Mason flustered, calls timeout."*

Before she knew it, the halftime buzzer was sounding. Erin flipped the notebook shut and stuck her pencil behind her ear. She stood up and stretched her arms.

"Off for the halftime interview?" asked Mr. Hardy.

"Hah! Fat chance!" groaned Erin. "Especially with the game this close."

"Sure is a nailbiter," agreed the teacher, looking over his partner's shoulder as she tallied up the stats. "Although it looked like we were going to put it away there at the beginning."

"Can I see that for a sec, Mrs. Trowbridge?" Erin pointed to the clipboard the other teacher held in her hand. "Looks pretty even," she said after glancing at the numbers. "They're even keeping right up with us on rebounds."

"Yes, indeed," said the teacher as she stowed her calculator in her book bag. "And they've brought their shooting percentage back up to almost 40 after missing those first six shots."

"Guess that's why it's a two-point ball game," commented Mr. Hardy. "Should be a wild second half!"

The Bobcats came out just as fired up as the Thunderbirds to open the second half. A quick score off the opening jump pulled the visitors into a tie. As the ball dropped through the net, Anna noticed a crowd of red uniforms fanning out in front of her. "Press!" she yelled as she stepped out of bounds with the ball.

Tina immediately sprinted back to help Jamie handle the inbound pass. Anna slapped the ball and tried to find an open passing lane, but both guards were covered. Eyeing Bernie stationed at midcourt, Anna pulled the ball back behind her head and launched a baseball pass. The perfectly targeted ball dropped right into the big center's outstretched hands ... and slipped through her fingers. Bernie's defender snatched up the fumble and flicked it ahead to a waiting teammate.

Jamie sprinted over to cover the ball, but her foot skidded on a patch of sweat. The Mason dribbler flashed past the off-balance guard. The layup gave the Bobcats their first lead since early in the second quarter.

The visitors' section roared their approval as the Bobcat press went into action again.

The Thunderbirds, alerted now, set up in their press-breaker formation. Anna calmly eyed the court. She pulled the ball back for another baseball pass, but caught the ball with her left hand just as she snapped it forward. The fake caught the Bobcat defenders leaning back up court, leaving an open lane for Anna to bounce a pass to Jamie. The point guard pivoted, saw the double team coming, and beat it with a quick pass across to Tina.

Anna raced ahead on the right as Tina dribbled up the middle. As the ball crossed the timeline, Jamie sprinted up to fill the lane on the left. Tina pulled up just before the free throw line. Her defender rocked back just a half step, anticipating a pass to Mollie under the basket. Room enough for Tina to launch a shot. Swish! Tie ball game.

The lead seesawed back and forth throughout the third quarter and into the fourth. Neither team could forge a lead of more than three. Players on both sides began hanging on to the legs of their shorts as they bent over whenever a whistle stopped play.

A 10-year-old ball girl under each basket was kept busy scrambling out to wipe up sweat from the floor with a towel at each break in the action. A flow of subs from both benches renewed the pace whenever it began to flag. Timeouts were called on both sides, as much for rest as for strategy. The clock ticked relentlessly down toward zero.

Jamie looked over at the bench. On a signal from the coach, she picked up her dribble. Cradling the ball in the crook of one elbow, she made a T with her hands. *"Timeout, gold!"* called the referee. Jamie tossed the ball to the official, then looked up at the scoreboard as she trotted over to the bench. Just 28 seconds to go. Down by three.

The coaches finished their quick conference, then turned to the waiting circle of players. Coach Miller knelt in the middle of the huddle. "Plenty of time, girls, plenty of time. Here's what we're going to do." She outlined three options on a half-court set play they'd been running in practice.

"We need to get off a good shot—a *good* shot, mind you—in 10–12 seconds. We don't need a three-pointer. In fact, what I want is a short jumper or layup, a high-percentage shot. Ten seconds should be plenty of time to work the ball around and get somebody open for a close-in shot. Then everybody—*everybody*—crashes the boards as soon as we get that ball through the basket, set up in a press—diamond and one, Amy on the inbounder. We're working for the turnover, but we can't waste too much time. A few seconds, then we have to foul."

The coach looked around the huddle, then made a decision. "McMahon, you're in for Behrens. Kiefer, you move over to the two spot. When we press, Anna, you're on Dutton—Number 15, the big shooter. I want you to face guard her, stay right inside her shirt. Johnson, shift over to help her out from behind if it looks like 15's going to go long. Don't let her get open for a pass. We can't afford to have to foul her. Anybody else, just not Dutton. She hasn't missed a free throw all night. Got it?"

Anna nodded. Jamie gave a thumbs-up. "OK," said the coach, holding out her hand. "On three, *believe!*"

Tina grabbed Barb's warm-up jacket as the senior shrugged it off her shoulders. "Get us to the playoffs, baby!" yelled Tina as Barb trotted over to the scorer's table to report into the game.

Jamie took the inbound pass from Anna and pushed the ball up the court. When she reached the top edge of the free throw circle, she hesitated. Seeing a zone, she gathered herself as if to shoot. Right on cue,

Amy dropped to the basket as her defender cheated up to help out on the shot. Lob pass. Bank shot. *Good!* Down by just one point now. And only eight seconds off the clock. Perfect. Twenty ticks to go. Still plenty of time.

The Mason center stepped out of bounds with the ball. Amy planted herself squarely in front of her, toes right up to the endline. Up and down she pogoed, waving her hands in the passer's face.

Anna turned to look back up the court. Quickly she located the red shirt marked 15, then stepped between her and the ball. Anna's eyes locked on her opponent's. Her feet shadowed her every move.

One second, two. Everybody covered. A frantic look on the passer's face. A whistle. *"Timeout, red!"*

"Perfect!" Coach Kelley clapped her hands as the subs leaped from the bench to engulf the five players racing off the court. "Just what we wanted. That was their last timeout, so this time we know they have to make the inbound pass. They'll be talking about our press during this timeout, so let's cross them up. We'll switch to a 2-2-1. Amy, you're floating back behind now, not up on the inbounder. You're free to double up if you anticipate a pass. Remember, now," she paused to look at Anna, "No fouls on Dutton."

Coach Miller picked up where her assistant left off. "We're only down by one point. And there's still 20 seconds left. Lots of time. Let's go for the steal first, or try to force a travel with a trap. But no more than 10 seconds, then we'll have to put them on the line. We need to get the ball back in time to get off a good shot, eight or nine seconds at least."

The head coach looked around the huddle once more. "All right, this is it!" She drew them in for their three-count cheer, then sent them back out on the floor.

The nervous Bobcats center took the ball from the referee, surprised this time to find her line of vision free of a jumping gold jersey. She held the ball in two hands over her head, searching for an open teammate. Got to get it in, got to find a hole ... somewhere. *There!*

She fired a chest pass to the corner. A split second too late, she caught sight of a skinny gold blur racing into the picture. Amy's outstretched hand just barely ticked the ball, deflecting the pass up into the air. The Bobcat receiver's hands clutched empty air. Behind her Mollie raced forward to leap at the ball as it headed out of bounds. Reaching, reaching ... Just missed it. Out of bounds. Just one second off the clock. Try again.

The Thunderbirds reset their press for the sideline inbound pass. A bounce pass got through this time. Another quick pass beat the Torrington trap. Sixteen seconds to go now. Fourteen. Twelve ...

Barb lunged to her left, reaching for the ball as the Bobcats played a desperate game of keep-away. Time to go for the foul.

Barb made contact with Number 24, hand against arm. But no whistle! Seven seconds, six ... A pass to the wing. Jamie stepped over to help Anna set a desperate trap. The whistle finally sounded.

"At the line, for Mason shooting one and one ..." crackled the announcer's voice over the screaming crowd, *"Number 15, Terri Dutton!"*

"Timeout!" yelled the Thunderbird coaches in unison.

Jamie pounded her fists on her head as she followed her teammates to the sideline. "Sorry, guys," she choked out. "I know we weren't supposed to foul Dutton. But I had to stop the clock."

"There's still four seconds left. It's not over yet!" Anna's voice startled Jamie from her funk. "Shake it off. You didn't have any choice."

"Yeah," echoed Barb. "We're not done yet. We're only down one. Even if she makes both free throws, we can still get a three, get it into overtime."

The coaches gave their instructions, then sent the team back out onto the court.

Five Thunderbirds crowded the lane lines as Mason's ace got set for her first try. Calmly, Number 15 went through her shooter's routine. Wipe the hands on the shorts, take the ball from the ref. Two measured dribbles, a relaxed stance. Up it goes. Looks good. It's got the range. *Swish!* A two-point lead. Groans from the crowd.

She's got the ball again. Bounce once, bounce twice, set, release. It's up, it looks good, it's heading down toward the rim... It's off! *She missed!* Three seconds to go, down by two...

Jamie snagged the long rebound as Barb raced ahead of her. A second ticked off the clock. The pass reached Barb in full stride, just as she crossed half court. She gathered it in, put down one quick dribble, then pushed up off her left foot, right knee driving up, giving force to the two-handed desperation three-point shot. The release just beat the buzzer ... but it's an awful long shot. It's up, it's on its way, it's ... it's ... *GOOD!*

A herd of screaming Thunderbirds piled onto Barb where she lay stunned on the court. "We did it!!" Jamie screamed into her ear as she pounded her on the back. "We won!" «

CHAPTER THIRTY-TWO

Torrington Faces Hunterville in Region Final

T-birds cruise through playoffs, face rivals in championship rematch

By Erin Melby
For the Torrington Times

BARNESVILLE—After giving their fans a major scare in the league showdown against Mason two weeks ago, Torrington has made winning look easy.

"Maybe we need the challenge of knowing that a loss means the end of our season," speculated senior co-captain Mollie Meyer. "Our teammates promised us three seniors they'd cap our last season with a regional championship, and now we're just one game away."

The district championship game last Friday with Plains Conference champ Farmington couldn't match the drama of the Valley Conference showdown with the Bobcats three days earlier. Torrington jumped to a 10-point lead over the Aggies by the end of the first quarter and never looked back.

"I told the girls my heart couldn't take another last-second thriller," joked Torrington skipper

Sharon Miller. "I guess they believed me."

The 81–57 win over Farmington vaulted the Thunderbirds into this week's three-game regional playoff at Munson Fieldhouse on the Shelby College campus in Barnesville.

"Playing at Shelby's almost like a home game for us," noted Miller. "I think that definitely gave us a boost in those first two regional games."

The first round on Tuesday pitted Torrington against perennial regional contender Harrisburg. Once again, a determined Thunderbird squad came out with guns blazing and rode the hot shooting of sophomore tandem Tina Behrens and Anna Kiefer to a double-digit halftime lead. Another strong performance by the Torrington bench extended the lead to as much as 25 before a too-little-too-late Harrisburg rally in the fourth quarter trimmed the final margin to 78–60.

In Thursday's semifinal, the Torrington

juggernaut rolled over District 4 champion Rock River 69–58. The Beavers managed to make it a contest in the early going. A trey by Rock River sharpshooter Jennifer Coleman broke a 21–all tie at 6:47 in the second quarter, but Torrington stormed back with a layup-plus-one by center Bernie Luskey. The Beavers never led again.

"We never really felt the game was out of reach," said Rock River coach Isabel Wheatly. "But every time we started to rally, Torrington would come up with a steal or a block or an offensive rebound and shut us back down."

Luskey and counterpart Amy Knudson combined for 26 points and 17 rebounds against Rock River while sharing post duties. Injured former starting center Millie Meyer lauded her replacements.

"We needed to find a way to take some of the pressure off Tina and Anna," Meyer said. "They'd been carrying most of the scoring load, and teams were starting to double up on them. That just opened up the middle, though, and Bernie and Amy came through for us big time."

Point guard Jamie Johnson posted a career high of 11 assists in the Rock River contest. Co-captain Barbara McMahon also contributed significantly off the bench, with season highs of 17 points and four steals.

Next up for the high-flying T-birds is a rematch with the ever-dangerous Hunterville Tigers. Torrington followers will surely recall their Thunderbirds' heartbreaking last-second loss to the Tigers in last year's regional final.

"We're a stronger team than when we met them last year," stated Miller. "We've been through some hard times this season, and that's galvanized this group. Last year we let Hunterville build a big lead on us in the first half. Even though we managed to dig ourselves out of that hole and had a chance to win the game, we were a little in awe of their reputation. Not this year. We respect them, but now we know we're on a par with them."

Hunterville coach Ian Evans agrees. "There's no underdog in this game this year. Torrington came of age with that near-win over Minneapolis Central in December, and they showed their maturity in this playoff stretch. We know we're in for a dogfight, but my girls are ready. We want another shot at a state championship next week, and we'll have to beat Torrington to get there."

Saturday's final is scheduled to tip off 30 minutes after the 2 pm consolation game pairing semifinal losers Rock River and Fullerton. For those unable to find tickets for the sold-out games, the action will be broadcast by KBAR (FM 97.5) and shown locally on cable television channel 23.

"Well, Maggie." said Mrs. Johnson, folding her newspaper and placing it next to her coffee cup. "Here we are again."

"You know, Katie," replied Mrs. McMahon, glancing around the bustling Friday lunchtime crowd at the Barnesville bagel shop, "I think we even sat at this same table for lunch the day before last year's Hunterville game!"

"Oh, dear! I hope it brings us better luck this time around. Maybe we should move to another table!"

Her companion laughed. "I'm afraid it's out of our hands now. Wonder how the girls are holding up?"

Mrs. Johnson wiped a bit of mustard from the corner of her mouth before replying. "Jamie has a math test this afternoon. Of all days…"

"Well, at least that might help her keep her mind off the game for a while!"

"I hope so," said Mrs. Johnson ruefully. "But knowing Jamie, it'll be the other way around." She glanced at the clock on the back wall. "Almost 1:00 already. I have to get back up the hill for my 1:30 class." She dug in her purse and laid some money on the table.

"Thanks for lunch," said Mrs. McMahon. "My turn next week."

"What time should we pick you up tomorrow?" asked Mrs. Johnson as she stood up from the table.

"Let's say 11:30. We'll want to get there a good hour before the first game if we want to get our usual seats."

The two women filed through the door and stood for a moment on the sidewalk outside. Mrs. McMahon picked up the conversation as she buttoned up her coat. "At least the state tournament tickets are reserved seating. If we make it past this game and into next week …"

"As the girls say, 'one game at a time,'" scolded Mrs. Johnson.

"I know, I know. But it's hard not to look ahead."

"Well, to be honest, I've already asked Karin if she can cover my classes next week."

"Aha!" said Mrs. McMahon. "So you're guilty, too!"

"Back to your store with you!" Mrs. Johnson commanded, smiling as she pointed to the gold-lettered shop door three stores away.

"See you tomorrow at 11:30 then."

"OK. Bye!"

With a quick hug, the two women parted. «

CHAPTER *THIRTY-THREE*

BEFORE THE GAME, the locker room was nearly deserted. Barb sat alone on a bench, smoothing the fabric of the gold uniform shirt draped across her knees. With her fingertip she traced the outline of the satiny blue number 22.

"You gonna put that thing on, or just sit there daydreaming all afternoon?"

The senior snapped out of her trance. Jamie stood in front of her, fully dressed, hands on hips, foot tapping.

"I was just thinking about all the times I've put this jersey on," said Barb.

The tone of her voice momentarily quieted Jamie's impatience. The toe tapping faded to silence in the empty locker room. Barb lifted her eyes to meet Jamie's. "It's been weird these last two weeks, thinking before each game how this could be the last time I get to wear it."

A sympathetic look flitted across Jamie's face, quickly replaced by a devilish grin. Jamie snatched the jersey off Barb's lap, gave it a furious shake, then tossed it back. "Well, it ain't gonna be today, Bucko," she said firmly. "You can worry about that *next* Saturday, when we're up at the Metrodome getting ready to play for the state championship!" The bravado in Jamie's voice brought a smile to her friend's face.

"C'mon, Slowpoke!" Jamie pulled Barb to her feet. "Let's get out there with everybody else and watch the end of the consolation game."

The two teams stood at the opening onto the fieldhouse floor. Jamie eyed her Hunterville counterpart, the orange number 10 outlined in white on the point guard's shiny black jersey. *"Left-handed,"* she reminded herself, going over the scouting report again in her head. Her eyes flicked over to Number 13 standing at the front of the pack of Tigers. Jamie frowned, remembering last year's long, last-second bomb that she'd launched over Jamie's head. The one that stole the victory that should have been theirs.

"Not this year!" she muttered fiercely under her breath.

"What'd you say?" asked Barb.

"Nothing," said Jamie, giving in to her pre-game jitter dance. "Let's get this show on the road!"

A buzzer-beating shot by Rock River mercifully saved the third-place game from stretching into overtime. "Whew!" Jamie exclaimed to Barb as they waited for the hand shaking to finish and the court to clear. "I don't think I could have lasted through another five minutes of that game."

"Hang in there, Jitterbug." Barb tugged Jamie's ponytail. "A few more minutes and you can unleash all that nervous energy on those poor, unsuspecting Tigers."

"I've been waiting a whole year for this day," came the reply. "Let me at 'em!"

« « « T » » »

As the Hunterville starters were being announced, Coach Kelley quietly pulled Jamie aside. "Watch for their defensive switches," she reminded the point guard. "They'll throw something different at us on each of the first few possessions, and you've got to read it and react."

"I know, Coach. I'm ready."

"And remember—"

"I know," Jamie interrupted. "No press till our first free throw, then hit them with the diamond and one. Don't worry, Coach. We've got it down."

Coach and player turned their attention back to the floor, where the final Tiger starter was sprinting out to join her teammates. The deafening roar of the crowd went on and on. Finally the announcer was able to make himself heard once again.

"And now, for the Torrington Thunderbirds, starting at guard, a junior, Number 11, Jamie Johnson!"

Jamie locked eyes for a moment with Barb. Barb gave Jamie's arm a squeeze, then pushed her out onto the court. A solid wave of sound carried Jamie to the middle of the floor. The noise crested four more times as each player was announced. Tina, Anna, Mollie, and finally Amy joined Jamie at center court. A thunder of applause kept them pinned where they stood.

Chaos dissolved into order as the first strains of the "Star-Spangled Banner" came from the band section. As cheers trumped the final note,

Millie dropped her right hand from her chest and held it out to her teammates. Eleven gold uniforms crowded around the tall figure in street clothes. "On three," Millie's already hoarse voice commanded, *"attack!"*

Hunterville's center had two inches and at least 30 pounds on Amy, but the freshman beat the Tiger to the tip, and Torrington was off to the races.

Jamie charged up the floor with the ball, scanning for a hole as the Tigers scrambled back on defense. She was still flying forward as she let go a pass to Amy, wide open under the basket. Jamie just had time to duck her shoulder before she crashed into her black-shirted defender. Oblivious of the falling bodies behind her, Amy hooked the ball over the rim and into the basket. Jamie landed hard, then rolled onto her back and grabbed her right ankle. A whistle stopped the action as Tina crouched over her fallen teammate.

"You OK?" asked Tina anxiously as she reached a hand down. Jamie grabbed it, levering herself gingerly to her feet. She tested the foot with a tentative step, then, more confidently, another.

"I'm fine," she said with relief.

"Foul, Number 11 gold—charging! Before the shot. No basket."

"What?" demanded Jamie, eyes flashing angrily at the ref.

"Cool it, Jamie," growled Mollie, grabbing the guard's arm. "Hustle back on defense. We'll get it back on the next one. You sure your ankle's OK?"

"I told you, it's fine," she spat as she backpedaled down the court. "But if that was a charge, I'll eat my ..."

The approach of the ball cut short the talk. Jamie set her mouth in a grim line. The Hunterville point guard dribbled in place as she surveyed the scene. Jamie inched forward, crowding the ballhandler's left side.

Quick as a flash, the lefty crossed over to her right hand and accelerated toward the basket. Jamie's hand flicked up from underneath, deftly and cleanly poking the ball away.

Tina saw the steal coming and was pushing off on a sprint to half court just as Jamie popped the ball loose. Tina caught up to the ball and pushed it ahead of her as she raced down the court. Anna flew up on her left. Jamie circled around to take the right lane. All clear ahead, three on none ... and ... was that another whistle?

"Reaching in, Number 11 gold!"

Jamie skidded to a stop, dropping her jaw in disbelief. She raised her eyes to the scoreboard. Less than 15 seconds off the clock, and a big red "2" was going up next to the number 11 on the home side of the big board.

A buzzer broke into her consciousness. Brenda approached from the scorer's table, holding out a warm-up jacket. Jamie groaned, then grabbed the jacket.

"Crappy call!" commiserated Brenda.

Jamie pursed her lips, bringing her venom under control. "Yeah, tough break. But we'll get past it." She patted her sub on the back. "Remember, watch for those switching defenses. Press on the first made free throw. You're the one now, Bren!"

The game resumed as Jamie plopped down next to Coach Miller. "Coach, I didn't—"

"I know, I know," the head coach said. "That charge call could've gone either way, but the steal was definitely clean. But that's the breaks, kiddo. I need you back in there, though, and soon, so shake it off."

Jamie turned her attention to the court. The Thunderbirds' 2-3 zone was holding solid against the Tigers' offense, clogging the middle and challenging the ball on the perimeter. The Tiger point guard pulled the ball back out a few dribbles, barking out a command as she held her right fist aloft.

The big Hunterville center flashed up to the high post, shadowed by Amy. A lob pass evaded the freshman defender's reach, and the Tiger center squared up to the basket. Amy recovered quickly, preventing a shot, but a pass to the wing found an open Tiger. Anna was there in an instant, but the shot was already away.

Up, down, good. First blood, Hunterville. 2–0 Tigers.

Anna picked up the ball and stepped across the endline. Four black shirts stayed in the backcourt with her. "Press!" Anna hollered. Seeing Brenda momentarily open, Anna didn't wait for the press-breaker to set up. Brenda gathered in the pass as two Tigers raced in her direction.

"*Pass it!*" screamed Jamie from the sideline. A moment of indecision, then Brenda put the ball on the floor. Nowhere to go, she picked it up again. Four hands darted up, blocking her vision. Brenda pivoted around, then back again before making a desperate heave over the outstretched hands. A waiting Tiger snatched the wounded duck out of the air. Pass, shot. 4–0, Tigers. And the press was on again.

Jamie squirmed on the bench next to Coach Miller. "Ready to get back in there, Johnson?"

"Yes, ma'am!"

"We can't afford a third foul on you before halftime, you know ... much less in the first quarter."

"I can do it, Coach. I promise!"

"OK. Next dead ball, you're back in for Thorson. Just remember—I'm counting on you to be our playmaker. Be smart out there!"

Jamie was already peeling off her jacket, crouching low as she ran along the sideline to kneel in front of the scorer's table. "11 in for 10!" she told the official scorer.

The game continued flowing up and down the court. Jamie went from kneeling to sitting, back to kneeling. Finally, a whistle!

"Good job, Bren!" she said as they made the exchange.

Brenda shook her head. "Watch for that trap on the press—it comes pretty fast!"

"Gotcha," replied Jamie as she turned to rejoin the action.

Two minutes before the half ended, Jamie was still on the floor. Barb was in now, and a whistle put her on the free throw line for a one and one. Jamie stepped up from behind her. "Put 'em both in, buddy. Give us the lead."

Barb mopped her forehead with her sweatbanded wrist, then took the ball from the ref. Bounce, bounce, bounce, pause. The set, the launch. Swish! Tie ball game.

A whistle shrilled as the crowd went wild. *"Timeout, black!"*

Jamie and Tina bracketed Barb as they jogged over to the bench. "Way to be cool, Barb," said Tina as she smacked palms with the forward.

"One more, baby!" added Jamie as she echoed the hand slap.

Coach Miller snared Jamie by the shirt as the trio neared the sideline. "Excellent work, Johnson!" the coach exclaimed. "I'm pulling you out for these last two minutes. Since you made it this far without getting your third, I don't want to press our luck before halftime."

After the huddle broke, Jamie looked for an open seat on the bench. "Way to hang tough out there, Jamie!" said Anna as she scooted down to make a space for the point guard.

"Thanks," came the muffled reply as Jamie wiped her face with a towel. "Nice job out there yourself."

Halftime came and went. Jamie finished retying her shoelace as the buzzer called the teams back onto the court. As she stood up to make her way out to the floor, Coach Miller checked her with a hand to the shoulder. "You sure that ankle's holding up OK?" asked the coach.

"It's fine," replied Jamie, bouncing up and down on her toes. "I can't even feel a twinge anymore."

"Good. We're going to need you out there this half, especially if they keep pressing. That 6–0 run while you were sitting before the half put us back in a bit of a hole."

"Don't worry, Coach. We're only down five. We'll get it back."

Amy won the toss again. Two passes later, Tina lofted a long shot from the left baseline, just beyond the three-point arc. Good! 38–36, Tigers by just two.

The teams traded baskets on the next two possessions. Next time down, the Torrington defense held its ground, forcing a bad shot. Mollie yanked down the rebound, then fired an outlet pass to the waiting Jamie. Jamie centered the ball as Anna and Tina raced to fill the outside lanes. Three on two.

The top defender backpedaled furiously, head swinging to check her left and right while she worked to slow Jamie down. Jamie pulled up at the top of the key, then pushed ahead again as the defender leaned left anticipating a pass.

Jamie drove hard to the basket. The back defender stepped up to meet her. Jamie released the ball just before the collision. All the way to the floor, she kept her eye on the basket. The ball kissed off the glass and into the basket. Uh-oh. Whistle.

"*Foul!*" said the ref, holding up her left hand as she pointed to the pair lying tangled on the floor.

Jamie held her breath.

"*Blocking, Number 13, black! Basket's good. One shot.*"

Jamie closed her eyes a moment, then breathed a long sigh of relief. She reached for Amy's outstretched hand.

"Close call," said the center as she started to pull the little guard to her feet.

"Yeah, don't scare us like that!" added Mollie as she tugged at Jamie's other hand.

Jamie looked up at the scoreboard as she walked to the line. All tied at 40, with 6:12 to go in the third. And still just that red 2 next to her number 11 in the home team's foul column.

Jamie calmly sank the free throw to give her team the lead. "Press!" she commanded as the ball sifted through the net. Five gold shirts sprinted into place as the vaunted Thunderbird full-court pressure clamped down on the Tigers.

Torrington slowly pushed their one-point lead to three, then five. A Hunterville three-pointer cut the margin to two. Anna answered with a three of her own. 55–50, Thunderbirds on top. Just under a minute to go now in the third quarter, Hunterville with the ball.

The Tigers patiently tested the Torrington zone with pass after crisp pass. The Thunderbird 2-3 shifted, shifted again. Thirty seconds. Twenty-five.

The ball swung back up top. Jamie moved with it. Twenty seconds. A fake shot. A jab step. Jamie stayed with her opponent move for move. The Tigers player whipped a chest pass to the wing.

Jamie took a step backwards, then scrambled back up as a quick return pass boomeranged back to the point. The shot went up as Jamie made a desperate swipe at the ball. The dreaded whistle sounded.

"On the arm, gold Number 11!"

The ball clanked harmlessly off the rim. Jamie raised her hand and looked reluctantly over to the bench. Brenda was already on her way to the scorer's table.

"Sorry, Coach," Jamie apologized as she took her seat on the bench next to the head coach.

"Don't worry about it, Johnson." Coach Kelley reached across her boss to pat Jamie on the knee. "You made it through almost three quarters with two fouls on you before picking up your third."

Coach Miller nodded, adding, "You just take a breather here for a bit, and we'll see how it goes in this last quarter. I don't want to risk you getting your fourth too early, but if they make a run at us, you be ready to go back in."

Jamie settled in to watch the action. The first free throw missed; the second was good. Four-point lead. Eight seconds to go in the third quarter.

Brenda was ready for the Tigers press this time, and she wasted no time working the ball ahead to Bernie at the center line. The Thunderbirds efficiently passed and cut, setting up the last shot for Anna on the wing. Anna beat the buzzer with a short jumper, and the ball dropped neatly through the cords. Thunderbirds by six. One quarter to go.

Midway through the fourth period, Jamie still sat on the bench. Amy went back in for Bernie. Barb spelled Anna. The Torrington lead stayed at six, dropped to four, crept back up to six, then stretched to eight.

Coach Miller eyed the scoreboard as the clock wound down to 1:00. Thunderbirds on top, 74–62. "Larson, you're in for McMahon!" shouted the coach. "And Swanson, in for Meyer."

As Emma and Jeri rose from the bench, Jamie looked hopefully at the coach. The coach smiled and shook her head. "Save it for next week, Johnson." Jamie shifted over to make room for Barb as she returned to the bench.

The roar grew as the Torrington crowd counted down the final seconds to the long-awaited win. Barb leaned over to yell in Jamie's ear. "I guess this isn't quite the way we pictured it all those years, eh? Fourth quarter of the regional finals, both of us on the bench."

"Hey, who cares?" exclaimed Jamie happily. "As long as we're winning." Jamie punched her pal on the arm. "Told you this wouldn't be the last time you wore that shirt. Metrodome, here we come!"

The final buzzer sounded and the victorious Thunderbirds sprinted towards the bench to celebrate their berth in the state tournament. Jamie reached into the duffel bag under her chair and pulled out something small and shiny.

"What's that?" asked Barb, catching a glimpse of silver metal.

"The scissors I've been carrying around all season," Jamie answered. "Let's go cut down those nets!" «

CHAPTER *THIRTY-FOUR*

JAMIE FLIPPED ON THE LIGHT in her bedroom and walked across to her desk. The chair was buried under an assortment of wrinkled clothes. Jamie shoved the pile onto the floor, then pulled out the chair and sat down.

She pushed aside several envelopes stuffed with state tournament pictures and negatives, a shoebox full of last season's newspaper clippings, and a stack of spiral notebooks. Her favorite pen emerged from the clutter. The small drawer at the front of the desk held a lined yellow tablet. Jamie set the pad of paper on the desk, then scrounged an envelope from the drawer before slamming it shut.

Friday, September 10, 1990 she wrote on the top of the page.

She stared at the empty space on the page in front of her. She tapped the pen on the desk, then stuck the end of it between her teeth. Her eyes wandered across the desktop to a sculpted wad of tinfoil. Perched atop the makeshift aluminum pedestal was the shiny green glass pea, its painted face smiling brightly. A basketball trophy stood behind it on the windowsill, adorned with a strand of whitish-gray net cord.

Jamie reached over to touch the gold-colored plate on the trophy's base. "1990 Region IV Champions" said the tag. Jamie smiled at the memories the trophy brought back. She pulled the pen from her mouth and began to write.

Dear Barb,

You know I'm not much of a writer, but I wanted to get a letter off to thank you for the cool sweatshirt you sent me. (It was in the mailbox waiting for me when I got home from school today.) I'd be willing to bet I'm one of maybe 10 people in all of southern Minnesota who's even heard of Lehigh University. (And probably the only one who knows it's in Pennsylvania!)

I wish you weren't quite so far away (or that I was smart enough to get into such a brainiac college next year ...), but I know that engineering scholarship was something you've always dreamed about. I'm glad to hear you decided to go to walk-on tryouts for the bball team. You know you'd miss having a team to hang out with and going to practice every day. (Call me as soon as you find out — I'll bet you make the team!)

Speaking of practice, the team's looking pretty good at captains' practices. It's kind of weird to be one of the ones running them this year, me and my trusty co-captains Jeri and Bernie. (I guess the team figured they had to vote for one midget to go with this year's version of the twin titans – ha!)

Seriously, though, the team is really starting to shape up already. I'd be surprised if Anna doesn't make All-State again this year, and Tina looks like she'll be right up there with her. There are three or four decent-looking freshmen and a couple of JV players who've really improved since last year. Coach Miller told us that the preseason coaches' and sportswriters' polls both have us ranked in the top five in the state, even after losing Millie and Mollie and you from last year's lineup. Talk about high expectations!

No matter what happens this season, though, there won't ever be another year like last year. All the ups and downs – almost beating the big city team in December, losing Millie in January (and almost our friendship…), getting that mid-season wakeup call with the two losses, coming back and beating Mason at the end to win the conference. Winning regionals, just like we planned. And of course that awesome trip to the state tournament!

I sure wish you were still around here to share it all with again. (Thanksgiving is way too far *away!) But we'll always have those memories of last year, and you know that no matter where we are, or whatever we end up doing, you'll always be my first and best friend.*

Wow – two pages! Guess that shows how much you rate!! Gotta go. Write soon!

Jamie signed her name with a flourish, then drew the outline of a Thunderbird underneath. She studied her sketch for a moment before adding a pair of lightning bolts flashing out of the bird's eyes.

She carefully ripped the two pages off the pad, then folded the letter, stuffed it in the envelope, licked the flap, and pressed it shut. She kicked back her chair and headed out to find a stamp.

On her way out of the room, she stopped to turn off the light. Her hand paused in midair as she saw the large wooden plaque on the wall. Jamie never got tired of reading the two-line inscription:

MINNESOTA STATE HIGH SCHOOL LEAGUE
1990 CLASS A STATE CHAMPIONS

ABOUT THE AUTHOR

JEANNE FOLEY grew up in Le Sueur, Minnesota back when playing organized basketball was just a dream for most girls. She was a math and physics major and co-captain of the women's basketball team at St. Olaf College in the early 1970s.

The enactment of Title IX during her college years launched Jeanne on a ten-year coaching career with stops at the University of Wyoming, Michigan Tech, the University of Michigan, Michigan State University, and Princeton University. After earning master's degrees in mathematics and kinesiology and a PhD in physiology, she spent nearly two decades teaching and conducting biomedical research at Michigan State University.

Jeanne was a charter member of the Women's Basketball Coaches Association in 1981 and was inducted as a Fellow in the American College of Sports Medicine in 1998. She currently resides in Menomonie, Wisconsin where she directs the Math Teaching and Learning Center at the University of Wisconsin-Stout. Jeanne's still a sports fan, though her recreational pursuits now tend toward biking, hiking and cutthroat Bananagrams.